THE CHRISTIAN BELIEF
IN IMMORTALITY

By

JAMES H. SNOWDEN

The Basal Beliefs of Christianity.

The World a Spiritual System.

Can We Believe in Immortality?

The Coming of the Lord.

Is the World Growing Better?

The Personality of God.

A Wonderful Night.

A Wonderful Morning.

The Making and Meaning of the New Testament.

Scenes and Sayings in the Life of Christ.

The Psychology of Religion.

A Summer Across the Sea.

The Truth About Christian Science.

The Meaning of Education.

The Attractions of the Ministry.

The City of Twelve Gates.

Jesus as Judged by His Enemies.

Sunday School Lessons, Four Annual Vols.

The
Christian Belief in Immortality
in the
Light of Modern Thought

BY

JAMES H. SNOWDEN

New York
THE MACMILLAN COMPANY
1925

Printed in the United States of America by
J. J. LITTLE AND IVES COMPANY, NEW YORK

PREFACE

In the summer of 1922, *The Churchman* announced that it would award a prize of $1,000 for the best treatise on the subject, "The Christian Belief in Immortality in the Light of Modern Thought." The contest, which was open to the world, closed on December 1, 1923. In the announcement the following statement appeared: "The characteristics to which the judges will pay most attention will be (1) Personal conviction, (2) Cogency of Argument and accuracy in statement of facts, (3) Literary Style.

Over one hundred manuscripts were submitted. The judges were the Rev. Francis A. Henry, D.D., of Morristown, New Jersey; the Rev. Elwood Worcester, D.D., of Boston, Massachusetts; and Dr. Walter Franklin Prince of New York City. These judges awarded the prize of $1,000 to the Rev. James Henry Snowden, D.D., of Pittsburgh, Pennsylvania.

GUY EMERY SHIPLER,
Editor, *The Churchman*.

CONTENTS

7

CONTENTS

If a man die, shall he live again?
I know that my Redeemer liveth,
And that he will stand at last upon the earth:
And after my skin, even this body, is destroyed,
Then without my flesh shall I see God.
                                        —*Job.*

The Universe is not dead and demoniacal, a charnel-house with spectres; but godlike, even my Father's.
On the roaring billows of Time, thou art not engulfed, but borne aloft into the azure of Eternity. Love not Pleasure; love God. This is the EVERLASTING YEA, wherein all contradiction is solved: wherein whoso walks and works, it is well with him.
                                        —*Carlyle.*

He who proclaims the existence of the Infinite—and none can avoid it—accumulates in that affirmation more of the supernatural than is to be found in all the miracles of the religions. For the notion of the Infinite presents the double character that it forces itself upon us and yet is incomprehensible. Through it the supernatural is at the bottom of every heart.
                                        —*Louis Pasteur.*

To me it seems that human life, small and confined as it is, and as, considered merely in the present, it is likely to remain even when the progress of material and moral improvement may have freed it from the greater part of its present calamities, stands greatly in need of any wider range and greater height of aspiration for itself and its destination, which the exercise of imagination can yield to it without running counter to the evidence of fact; and that it is a part of wisdom to make the most of any, even small, probabilities on this subject, which furnish imagination with any footing to support itself on.
                                        —*John Stuart Mill.*

For we know that if the earthly house of our tabernacle be dissolved, we have a building from God, a house not made with hands, eternal in the heavens.
                                        —*Paul.*

9

THE CHRISTIAN BELIEF
IN IMMORTALITY

THE CHRISTIAN BELIEF IN IMMORTALITY IN THE LIGHT OF MODERN THOUGHT

CHAPTER I

INTRODUCTION

1. *The Need of Reëxamining the Question.*

The belief in immortality is one of the oldest and most universal faiths in the world. One of the oldest books in existence is the Egyptian *Book of the Dead*, all ancient Egyptian literature and life were saturated with this belief, and primitive literature in every language and the most ancient human remains bear witness to this faith.

It might be supposed, then, that this belief, which, as Voltaire said, has been "discussed for four thousand years in four thousand ways," would now be so surely established, or else so thoroughly discredited, that it would need no further examination and discussion. Will the world never reach certainty and finality on so vital a question?

The answer is that all questions are ever open to and call for new investigation and evaluation. Every generation must solve for itself all the old as well as the new

13

problems and settle its own doubts as certainly as it must cut its own clothes and breathe through its own lungs. Finalities are never reached in any field, not even in physics and mathematics, and increasing knowledge keeps all questions open and exposes them to fuller light and further modification. All new knowledge reacts upon the old and they must be mutually adjusted into harmony.

All our beliefs have thus been disturbed down to their deepest roots by the immense modern expansion of our knowledge. The atom that only a few years ago was believed to be an ultimate and indivisible entity has now been literally blown to pieces and is known to be as complex and wonderful and mysterious as the solar system. Relativity, according to its adherents, has not spared our most fundamental and solidly settled beliefs as to the constitution of the physical universe. It has discarded the old and formulated a new law of gravitation, and has wrecked the supposedly fixed and rigid framework of space and time and set them afloat on the sea of change. All our beliefs, even the oldest and most sacred, have moved into a new world of inquiry and are open to further discussion and revision.

It is not surprising, then, that the ancient belief in human immortality has shared in the spirit and changes of the new age and is now being debated more seriously and earnestly and urgently than ever before. This is not a sign of weakness and of withering worth, but simply shows that it is a human belief and partakes of the processes of human thought; and the fact that it has lasted so long and passed through so many fluctuations and crises in this world of change is greatly in its favor

as showing that it has in it some inherent and indestructible truth and value.

We are not, therefore, afraid or hesitant in the presence of the ever recurring need of reëxamining this belief
and enter upon the inquiry with a determination to
subject it anew to critical investigation and learn as far
as we can the truth about it.

2. *What Is the Christian Belief in Immortality?*

We should begin our discussion with an understanding
of the meaning of our terms. Belief in immortality
assumes many forms. Some things pass under this name
that are not worthy of it and really have no right to it.

Any pantheistic form of immortality that merges the
individual personality in the general unconscious soul
and sea of the universe does not answer to the great
need and demand of human life and "is faith as vague as
all unsweet," and does not concern us in this discussion.

The attempted substitution for personal immortality
of "the immortality of influence," which has found classi-
cal and eloquent poetic expression in George Eliot's
Choir Invisible, is another form of this faith which
makes a promise to the ear and breaks it to the heart.
However it may appeal to some minds, as is seen in
Professor Kirsopp Lake's recent Ingersoll Lectures on
Immortality and the Modern Mind, such minds are ex-
ceptional; it is a view that does not fulfill any proper
meaning of immortality, and it falls outside the field of
our subject.

Any form of immortality worthy of the name is the
permanence of human personality after death. This is
what is meant by this word the world over and the ages

through and is the only faith that will satisfy the human mind and heart. These pantheistic and social forms are only phantom shapes, and in endeavoring to find faith and comfort in them we are only hugging delusions which can no longer delude us after they have been found out.

Our concern is with the Christian belief in immortality, and this is set forth in the Christian Scriptures, especially in the New Testament and more definitely still in the teaching of Christ himself.

This Scripture teaching is clear and positive as to the main point, and yet shadowy in general outline and meager in detail of content. The clearest and fullest expression of it is Christ's own teaching in the opening verses of the fourteenth chapter of the Gospel by John: "Let not your heart be troubled: believe in God, believe also in me. In my Father's house are many mansions; if it were not so, I would have told you; for I go to prepare a place for you. And if I go and prepare a place for you, I come again, and will receive you unto myself; that where I am, there ye may be also." These memorable words have lost none of their music and charm after the lapse of nineteen centuries and are still an authoritative and unequalled expression of the Christian belief in immortality.

Paul states his view of this hope in his "desire to depart and be with Christ; for it is very far better" (Phil. 1:23). John gives his view in the third chapter of his First Epistle: "Beloved, now are we the sons of God, and it is not yet made manifest what we shall be. We know that, if he shall be manifested, we shall be like him; for we shall see him as he is."

INTRODUCTION

In the Apocalypse of John the descriptions of the city of God, some of which relate to this city as it is rising on earth and others to the eternal city in heaven, are obviously pictorial and are not to be pressed into literality. But here, also, we are given glimpses of a perfect society of redeemed spirits. The writer of Hebrews tells us that we "are come unto mount Zion, and unto the city of the living God, the heavenly Jerusalem, and to innumerable hosts of angels, to the general assembly and church of the firstborn who are enrolled in heaven, and to God the Judge of all, and to the spirits of just men made perfect, and to Jesus" (12:22-24).

To these Scriptural descriptions of the heavenly life must also be added the idea of service: "And his servants shall serve him" (Rev. 22:3). An immortality of eternal idleness would soon make us tired and become intolerable. We are made for activity and service in every faculty of our being and such employment is necessary to our satisfaction. As this urge of the soul is constitutional it will never be spent but will demand an appropriate field of action and service through eternity. The immortal life will be our earthly life raised to ever higher degrees of perfection and power. Of the good man it may be affirmed,

> He asks no isles of the blest, no quiet seats of the just,
> to rest in a golden grove, or to bask in a summer sky;
> Give him the glory of going on and not to die.

These teachings may be summarized as meaning the permanence after death of conscious personality living in enduring friendship and worthy service.

This general form of the New Testament doctrine has

17

been elaborated and embroidered in Christian theology and teaching and literature, especially in Christian hymns and most of all in "Gospel songs," so that it has been overloaded with details and concrete descriptions that go far beyond the meager outlines of Christ and his apostles into a richly-colored, highly-heated region of imagination; and these fanciful pictures have resulted in a materialistic and luscious sentimental heaven in which we are to live in luxurious ease and passionate love and "sing ourselves away in everlasting bliss," and such a heaven becomes repellent and offensive to many right-thinking minds.

We are not committed to any such immortality in this discussion. The New Testament writers and especially Christ himself teach a definite undoubting faith in a future life of blessed friendship, but refrain from such uninviting and embarrassing details. The life beyond this world of time and space and sense into which flesh and blood cannot enter and which it is not possible for us even to conceive, would not be understandable by us, however its portals might be thrown open to us through the dim windows of our human words that are all set in the frames of sense. It may be that our future existence will be some form of that "immortality in God" which some philosophers, such as Royce, set forth. Such a view is not exclusive but may be inclusive of the Christian belief in immortality so long as it does not absorb human personality in God but maintains its conscious existence in the Father of spirits. Such questions lie beyond the range of the present discussion.

There are also other subordinate questions and special aspects of our subject, such as conditional immor-

tality, whether eternal life is a constitutional principle
and inherent actuality of the human soul and therefore
the common possession and destiny of all souls, or
whether it is only a capacity and opportunity to be developed and realized, a goal to be gained, and therefore
only a possibility which only some will attain; and such
questions do not fall within our specified field. Conditional immortality is held by many able advocates of
the Christian belief in immortality and is a recognized
form of it, but this question does not belong to this discussion. Our sole problem is how the general principle
and not specific forms of it stand in the light of modern
knowledge.[1]

3. *What Is Modern Thought?*

Our subject also requires us to determine what is meant
by modern thought and to consider what is its relation to
Christian belief in immortality. There is much true
thought that is not modern, for wisdom did not begin
with us moderns, and there is also much that passes
under the name of modern thought that is not thought
at all in any worthy sense. The phrase is a broad and
general one, and yet it has definite meanings.

(1) It means, first, the great mass of new knowledge
that has been accumulated in modern times. In the last
hundred years a hundred sciences have been born and

[1] Conditional immortality has recently received the weighty support of Professor Pringle-Pattison in his *The Idea of Immortality*
and of Professor James Y. Simpson in his *Man and the Attainment of Immortality.* An elaborate and learned discussion of
the leading theories of immortality will be found in *The Problem of Immortality,* by R. A. Tsanoff, published by the Macmillan Company, 1924.

grown into giant power. Biology, anthropology, embryology, psychology, genetics, eugenics,—we need only mention such names to suggest the new world of knowledge.

All the old sciences have been rewritten and almost reconstituted. The new astronomy has thrown the old into the shade and outdazzled it beyond the dreams of the older astronomers. Herschel declared that there was one thing astronomers would never know, the diameters of the stars, for no telescope can disclose their disks, but now we can know them and the high school scholar can understand the process by which these diameters are determined. The astronomers formerly told us of things they saw that frightened us: now they see things that frighten them. They now know they are only touching the fringes of the constellations and are far from the borders of the universe and appreciate the Psalmist's exclamation: "Lo, these are but the outskirts of his ways: and how small a whisper do we hear of him!"

History is being rewritten and is giving us new light on the most ancient times and is penetrating deeper into the course and causes of all human events. Evolution has revolutionized every field of knowledge. The Bible has been passed through the process of higher criticism and has come out a very different book from former conceptions of it.

This new knowledge has accumulated in vast heaps and masses on every field. And now every old belief must be adjusted into harmony with it. For one of the surest intuitions and most certain beliefs of the human mind is the unity and consistency of all truth. We cannot tolerate any contradiction or break or disharmony in the universal web and structure of reality, but instinctively and irresistibly believe that all truths must run into one system and cohere in unity as all radii of a circle run to and meet in one center.

Religion and science must then get together, and where there is conflict apparent or real, the one or the other or both must be modified until they match and merge into harmony.

This has been an age-long process and is a persistent battlefield in which old religion has often mistakenly opposed new science and has at last been forced to come into agreement with it. The conflict over the Copernican astronomy and modern geology need only be mentioned as illustrations. Sooner or later religion and science do come together in mutual consistency, and then their relations go on smoothly and comfortably to faith until some new revolutionary scientific truth arises, when the process of conflict and adjustment is again repeated.

The Christian belief in immortality is now in contact with all this modern knowledge. It must adjust itself to it, or it cannot survive. The truth that is in it must be wrought into harmony with the truth that is in anything and everything else, and this belief would refuse to do this at the peril of its life. It cannot shut itself up in a cell and maintain itself in isolation from and against the opposition of all other knowledge. Our minds are not constructed in water-tight compartments so that we can believe with one faculty or part of our knowledge what we disbelieve with another. In particular, we cannot continue to believe with our hearts what we deny with our heads; and we cannot permanently retain in our hearts feelings, however sacred, that have been discredited before the bar of reason in the brain. Every belief must come out into the light of all our knowledge and live in the day in harmony with all other beliefs.

The Christian belief in immortality can have no discharge in this war, can claim or ask no special privileges on the ground of its sacredness, but must fight its battle and take its chance in the open field of modern knowledge.

(2) Modern thought means, second, a new spirit of inquiry, the scientific spirit of truth-seeking, the idea and aim and endeavor of simply reaching reality and knowing the truth on any and every subject. It is true that this spirit was recognized and used in some degree in former times, even in the ancient world. Socrates was keenly skilful in practicing this method, and Aristotle followed it. The writers of the Bible and the founders of Christianity were not unacquainted with it. Jesus preëminently incarnated it and declared, "I am the truth."

Nevertheless it has been emphasized and pushed into prominence and dominance in our modern world as the most characteristic principle and spirit of its thought. Now the thorough and pitiless search for truth is our direct aim and urgent endeavor. Everything must go into the crucible and the fire of investigation. Tradition and sacredness are not cloaks and masks that can conceal and protect anything. The scientific spirit will ruthlessly tear off such means of secrecy or evasion and expose whatever is within and behind them. Even an ancient Hebrew king said unto the prophet, "Speak unto me nothing but the truth" (I Kings 22:16), and this is the text of our modern thought. The "cry for reality" is the dominant note of our day.

We have an intuition and instinctive belief that only the truth is good and will do us good in the end. No lie can last. Falsity is rottenness at the root that will cause its scarlet blossoms to go up in dust. Modern thought has a severe and solemn creed on the subject of truth. It holds as the first article in its confession of faith that truth is the primary duty and virtue of the human mind, the chastity and fine bloom of the soul, and that untruth, especially when due to any lack of mental honesty or thorough inquiry on our part, is a fundamental sin.

The Christian belief in immortality must also be critically tested by this principle of modern thought. It cannot claim any immunity under the cloak of its consecrated sacredness. It must unreservedly submit itself to the most searching examination and abide by the consequences. If this belief is unfounded and untrue, we ought to want to know it. Tell us the truth on this subject though our heaven of hope comes crashing down and leaves only a blank void and starless night after death. But if this faith has deep and secure foundations, the pick and shovel and dynamite of modern thought will only uncover and assure us of these foundations and make our faith more confident and comforting.

The question of how stands our Christian belief in immortality in the light of this modern thought will be considered in the following pages.

4. *The Methods and Results of Our Study.*

The methods of our inquiry are those which are used in all fields of knowledge, especially in the region of ethics and religion. Intuition, perception, collecting all available facts, comparison and classification, combination of ideas and objects into larger units, tracing of causal links and connections, the use of analogy, the deduction of principles and their wider application, constructive thought and imagination, all the means and methods of experience apply to this problem and lead us toward its solution. Impartial scientific care and caution should be exercised in the use of these means. Prejudice and dogmatism, superficial reasoning and hasty conclusions, should be studiously avoided, and we should proceed under a solemn sense of the primary duty of truth.

The trustworthiness of the human mind, when critically used, as an organ of knowledge is an assumption which must underlie this undertaking, as it does all our reasoning in any field. We must trust something before we can know anything, and the mind must trust itself or it cannot prove or disprove anything. If it cannot know that it is trustworthy, then it cannot know that it is untrustworthy, and all knowledge is at an end. From a very small base on the earth the astronomer determines the distance of the sun and stars, and from a seemingly small area of thought in the brain the mind dares to think its way up to God and catch a vision of the life immortal.

This process, however, must not be confined to the cold region of pure reason. Reason has its place and must be heard in this discussion, but there are also other

24

and deeper voices in us that must be allowed to speak. The heart is older than the brain and has something to say on all the practical questions and great issues of life. The whole personality, intellectual, affectional and volitional, its constitutional intuitions and spiritual insights and mystic yearnings, as well as its logical processes, must speak on this question. Any claim of physical science or of formal logic to be the only or the final voice in the region of religion and immortality cannot be allowed. "Taking truth as a whole," says Lotze, a profound thinker and impressive authority in this field, "we are not justified in regarding it as a mere self-centered splendor, having no necessary connection with those stirrings of the soul from which, indeed, the impulse to seek it first proceeded. On the contrary, whenever any scientific revolution has driven out old modes of thought, the new views that take their place must justify themselves by the permanent or increasing satisfaction which they are capable of affording to those spiritual demands, which cannot be put off or ignored." [2]

The first and final word on this subject is faith. This is not to base our hope on an untrustworthy or illegitimate kind of belief, for after all our reasoning on any subject we must fall back upon this primal and fundamental principle. We begin and end with faith in all our beliefs and actions. Primal instincts and impulses push us into action before we reason about them. "Man is endowed with reason," said Benjamin Franklin, "in order that he can give reasons for what he wants to do," and "the heart has reasons," said Pascal in his well-known words, "which reason does not know."

[2] *Microcosmus*, Introduction, p. IX.

25

THE CHRISTIAN BELIEF IN IMMORTALITY

All the really great things in life and the world are matters of faith. "By faith we understand that the worlds have been framed by the word of God, so that what is seen hath not been made out of things which appear." By faith the scientist trusts his senses and instruments and reasoning processes, trusts the universality of law and the rationality of the universe, and looks backward to primal cells and molten globes, and forward to cooling planets and coffined worlds. "As for the strong conviction," says Huxley, "that the cosmic order is rational, and the faith that, throughout all durations, unbroken order has reigned in the universe, I not only accept it, but I am disposed to think it the most important of all truths." See how boldly he plants himself on "faith"! Verily this eminent man of science and chief agnostic of his day has become one of the prophets and shows greater faith than is often found even in Israel. If science must exercise this mystic power of the mind and heart with reference to the physical world, it cannot forbid or discourage but must greatly encourage us in using this same power with reference to the spiritual and eternal world.

By faith Columbus discovered a new world, and Luther shattered religious despotism, and Lincoln liberated a fettered race. By faith men of genius see visions and write them into poems and carve them into statues, and build them into cathedrals, and paint them in pictures, and sing them in songs, or work them out in revolutionary inventions, or spread them out across continents in empires or republics. By faith prophets have foreseen the slopes and summits of future achievements and victories and unveiled their glory to the world. By

26

faith martyrs and soldiers have given their blood for the blessing of coming generations. Could we remove faith from the world we would undermine and throw down its corner foundation stone and its central column and let its whole structure fall into ruins.

Faith is a step into the unseen and implies some risk and courage. It is an adventure that tries the soul and turns its trial into triumph. Were it possible to take all faith out of our life and reduce it all to sight and certainty, we would thereby level the heights of aspiration and inspiration, sweep all visions out of our sky, and lower life to a dull routine of mechanism and drudgery. The animal has no factor of faith and hope in its instinctive life, "the present only toucheth it," but man faces the unknown future that is the field of his problems and possibilities, the ocean on which his "purpose holds to sail beyond the sunset, and the baths of all the western stars." There would be no surprise and wonder, venture and courage, vision and victory in a world without faith. The power of faith is one of the marks of the greatness of man, and death gains infinite interest and worth from the fact that it is man's sublimest adventure.

The conclusion we can reach on this subject is one of probability. Few of our results are of any other degree of assurance, and only in mathematical demonstrations do we reach absolute certainty, and even this is doubted by some recent thinkers. All our practical conclusions rest on probability of greater or less degree. And such knowledge answers our practical purposes, and we act upon it with full confidence. Once the balance turns towards one side of probability, we throw our whole weight upon it and commit our all to it.

THE CHRISTIAN BELIEF IN IMMORTALITY

We may not demonstrate our faith in immortality so as to put it beyond the doubt of sceptical minds or even of our own minds, but we may reach it along converging lines of evidence and reason which meet in a focus of faith that becomes a practical assurance and guidance in action.

> We have but faith: we cannot know;
>   For knowledge is of things we see;
>   And yet we trust it comes from thee,
> A beam in darkness: let it grow.
>
> *—Tennyson.*

CHAPTER II

MODERN VIEWS OF THE UNIVERSE

Science has wrought Copernican revolutions and continental and climatic changes in the intellectual world, shifting its center and lifting or lowering its continents and mountain ranges and thus producing changes of climate that have caused some forms of thought to grow into bloom and fruitage and others to wither and become obsolete or extinct. It has given life and power to some religious doctrines and left others embedded as fossils in the mental strata of our modern world.

How has the Christian belief in immortality been affected by these changes? There are several points at which modern scientific and philosophical views bear upon this faith.

1. *The Vastness of the Universe.*

The first of these is the vastness of the universe. The former conceptions of the expanse of the heavens, great as they were, have been enormously extended by the revelations of our modern instruments. The microscope, telescope, spectroscope, photographic camera, and interferometer are in effect immense eyes that enable us to peer into the world of matter in both directions. The microscope opens vistas into the infinitesimally small, the telescope into the unimaginably distant and great,

29

the photographic camera looks with a fixed and steady eye and accumulates light and thus photographs stars and nebulæ no telescope can reveal, the spectroscope reports the chemical composition, motion, direction, speed and distance of stars, and the interferometer measures their diameters.

These enormous eyes, gazing with steady stare through hours at the heavens and fixing their reports in permanent form, have disclosed a universe which is an inconceivably vast whirling snowstorm of stars and systems of such dimensions, distances and speeds as bewilder and appall us. There are huge solar monsters, such as Betelguese with a diameter of 240 million miles, and Antares with a diameter of over 400 million miles so that if our sun were placed at the center of Antares our earth would be something like 100 million miles within the star. Our sun could be dropped into one of its spots or yawning chasms as we drop a pebble into a well.

The light-year, which is the distance traveled in a year by a ray of light moving 186,300 miles a second, is the yardstick with which the astronomer measures the distances of the heavenly bodies, and some stars are many thousands and possibly millions of light-years away.

Most mysterious and terrifying of all are the star clusters and nebulæ which are vast dust heaps and sand shores of stars and nebulous matter sprawling over inconceivable regions of space; and more amazing still are the spiral nebulæ which are thought by some astronomers to be "island universes" lying outside our universe or galaxy at distances immense compared with the distance of the stars, repeating, we know not how many times and on what vaster scales, the wonders of our own. The Great Magellanic Cloud, in the southern hemisphere, is believed to be such a universe many billions of times as far away as our sun so that the light by which we now see it left it hundreds of thousands of years ago. Our own galaxy, which has the general shape of a disk, is estimated to be three hundred thousand light-years in diameter and four thousand light-years thick. The total number of the stars, formerly put at a hundred millions, has now gone up into billions.

These inconceivable magnitudes and distances are also matched by equally inconceivable ages of time, so that millions of years are only as one day in the calendar of the heavens or as a single tick of its mighty clock. Even the age of our own planet is now variously estimated at from a hundred million to several billion years, and if the geological ages be represented by twelve hours on the face of a clock the whole period of human history would be represented by the last ten seconds of these twelve hours.

The terror of such conceptions is greatly increased when we are told to view the universe as boundless space swarming with inconceivable numbers of suns and systems in all stages of evolution and passage from life to death and from death to life. They are, either through nebular condensation or solar collisions, kindling and bursting into luminosity and white heat with trains of planets cooling into continents and blooming into life, and then slowly freezing, ruthlessly extinguishing all life and becoming coffined in ice, to swing silent and dark and dead in their orbits until some new collision or other catastrophe causes them again to blaze out in the sky

31

and starts them on another cycle in the endless round
of life and death.

The first effect of such conceptions of the heavens is
to dwarf our earth into a mere mote floating in this
shoreless sea of night sprinkled with splendor and then
still further to dwarf man into this "fretful midget" and
the human race itself into a minute ant-hill troubled in
"the gleam of a million million suns." And what matters it, then, says a pessimistic writer, how often these
ants fight and what becomes of them?

And what becomes of the human soul under all this
weight and crush of matter? Is it not simply smothered
into a single gasp of breath, or snuffed out like a tiny
candle or fitful spark in a storm?

The case, however, is not so alarming as it may seem,
for the first appearance of things is often deceptive,
and the difficulty dissolves under reflection. On any
theory of philosophy matter cannot overtop and crush
mind, whatever its mass and weight. Man himself thinks
the universe, and thereby rises above it and puts it
under his feet. However vast he discovers it to be, it
is his own mind that perceives and reconstructs its star-
fretted dome, he sets it all up in his own brain and
thereby subordinates it to himself. At once he imposes
upon it the principles of his own thought and bids all
its stars and systems wheel into the orbits and around
the centers of his own laws of unity and harmony and
causal connection. He thus commands it to obey him,
and it comes creeping to his feet and kneeling before
him. He erects his throne in its midst and rules over
it with a scepter that reaches to its inmost atom and its
farthest frontier. Idealistic philosophy dissolves the

32

whole material universe into a manifestation of mind or a spiritual system which is the content of an Infinite Mind and in which our finite minds share. On any world view, incomparably the greatest and most wonderful star is at the little end of the telescope, the star of the human mind that is looking, not the star that is being looked at.

Thus the soul of man rises regnant in the midst of the vastness of the universe, and the greater it is, the greater he is. Such a being is of incomparably higher rank and worth than infinite masses of matter and has a right to outlast all the stars.

> The stars shall fade away, the sun himself
> Grow dim with age, and nature sink in years,
> But thou shalt flourish in immortal youth,
> Unhurt amidst the wars of elements,
> The wrecks of matter, and the crush of worlds.
> —*Addison.*

2. *The Universality of Law.*

Another modern scientific doctrine bearing on the immortality of the soul is the universality of law. Science is the search for order and harmony and final unity, and it finds these as it extends the reign of law. Nature at first sight presents the appearance of confusion and chaos, and men have slowly threaded their way through its jungle and cleared it up into law and system. The physical world has been widely brought under this principle, and now it is believed, though this belief is an immense exercise of faith, that law reigns down to the last atom and electron of the universe.

The same principle has been extended to the mental and moral and spiritual world, though there is some distinction between physical and ethical laws, the latter involving a voluntary element. Human souls, however, are not capricious beings forming a chaotic social order, but are law-saturated organisms cohering in an orderly system.

This extension of the reign of law, until it has become coterminous with the whole field of being, at first seems to reduce personality to mechanism and thereby to imprison and destroy its essential nature of moral freedom and responsibility. As law was extended over each additional area it seemed that both man and God, considered as free beings, were driven out of that field and shut up in a narrower sphere in which to act and exist, and that finally they were crowded out of the law-ruled universe altogether. God, according to this view, has thus become imprisoned in his own world, and his personality has been rendered impotent and has been destroyed, and much more has man lost his personality in the same irresistible process. Undoubtedly the reign of law has made it seem more difficult for the modern mind to believe in either the personality of God or the freedom of man.

But again the difficulty is greatest at first view, and abates and disappears under reflection. In the case of man he clearly exercises his conscious freedom in a world of physical laws. He does not and cannot violate them, but he combines and turns them to his own ends, and this is what he is doing in all his mastery of nature. Physical energies have increasingly become his nimble servants, so that he hitches his wagons to the great golden driving wheel of the sun and rides in ease and comfort. He is wholly environed in physical energies, and yet they no more fetter and impede him than does his own skin which constantly adapts itself without friction or hindrance to all his activities and aids him in them.

Man is not imprisoned in nature, but in a degree is its master and lord. The universe with all its laws is his servant, and its powers bow to his personality at every step. Man is a supernatural being and moves through nature in the full possession and exercise of his freedom. Laws are the means of his liberty, the grooves and guides in which his liberty moves with smoothness in speed and safety. The steel track does not destroy the liberty of the locomotive but gives it all the liberty it has. Law and liberty are not antagonistic but are mutually complementary and harmonious. It is because man lives in a world of law that he can have liberty and life.

Lotze wrote his monumental work, *Microcosmus*, to show "how absolutely universal is the extent, and at the same time how completely subordinate the significance, of the mission which mechanism has to fulfill in the structure of the world." And Mr. A. J. Balfour, in his Gifford Lectures on *Theism and Humanism*, speaking of the difficulties in connection with natural law and prayer, says: "These difficulties are difficulties of theory, not of practice. They never disturb the ordinary man—nor the extraordinary man in his ordinary moments. Human intercourse is not embarrassed by the second, nor simple piety by the first. And perhaps the enlightened lounger, requesting a club waiter to shut the window, brushes aside, or ignores, as many philosophical puzzles as a mother passionately praying for the safety of her child."

Man, then, moves through the universe, and its laws

are not weights but wings to his freedom and personality; and equally the ethical laws of his character are an expression of his liberty and life. Personality finds its proper field and exercise, not in caprice, but in plan and purpose; and thus the reign of law in the universe, instead of being an objection and fatal obstacle to the personality of man and the immortality of his soul, is rather the necessary condition of his freedom and of his great hope.

3. *The Theory of Evolution.*

A third modern doctrine that bears upon our problem is the theory of evolution. This now dominates the whole field of thought and is applied to physical nature from the ether to atoms and molecules, and from nebulæ to suns and systems, and in the biological world to life from single-celled organisms up to man. Its central principle is that of genetic connection and continuity as the simpler forms unfold into the more complex, and it also includes a reversal of the process in devolution.

This central principle is now universally accepted in the scientific world, though the mechanism or factors of the process are still an unsolved problem. Darwin's theory of natural selection is now generally held to be an inadequate explanation of evolution and efforts are being made to find the determining cause in the secret of heredity.

So revolutionary and dominant an idea was bound to be attended with mistaken views in its interpretation and application, and at first sight it seemed to many to be destructive of all worthy ideas of divine creation and providence and of human personality and immortality.

But continued reflection has cleared up such views and showed that the theory leaves all these problems unaffected in their essential nature, though throwing new light upon them. The fundamental fact as to evolution is that it is a method and not a cause. It only shows how causes work, but does not account for the causes themselves. It cannot bring out explicitly in the result anything that was not implicit in the beginning or was not put into the course of the process. If any increment comes out in the product that was not in the cause, such an increment would be an event or effect without a cause, and this would contradict one of the most fundamental of our axiomatic intuitions. That every event has a cause is a necessary belief that lies embedded in the foundation of all our thought and action and applies to the whole creation from the beginning to the end.

This point was brought out and sharply emphasized in an address on evolution delivered before the American Association for the Advancement of Science in Toronto, Canada, December 21, 1921, by Professor William Bateson, an eminent English biologist and thorough-going evolutionist. He contended that "the claims of natural selection as the chief factor in the determination of species have consequently been discredited," and that "the variations to which interspecific sterility is due are obviously variations in which something is apparently added to the stock of ingredients," and declared that a new species is "a variation in which something has been added."

This recent authoritative word of evolutionary science is in strict accord with an old account of the origin of man: "And Jehovah God formed man of the dust of the ground, and breathed into his nostrils the breath of life; and man became a living soul" (Gen. 2:7). *"The breath of life"* and *"a living soul"* was "the something added to the stock of ingredients" in the evolutionary origin of man, and in the light of the latest biological science this record stands

Evolution, then, is only a method and is a description of the way all causes work back and up to the First Cause in God. It is the divine program of creation, written broadly across the first chapters of Genesis and expressed in all the processes of the world. Being the plan and program of God, it does not in the least impair his freedom and hamper his presence and purpose in the world. So far from destroying or crippling his personality, it gives full and free expression to it, and equally does it leave room for the personality and freedom of man and for his immortality.

Not only does evolution not stand in the way of human immortality, but, as in the case of the vastness of the universe and the reign of law, it turns out to be an argument in its favor. For evolution ever leads up to higher forms and finally culminates in personality in man, and this fact points on to his permanent personality. We cannot think that evolution would struggle so long and slowly at so great cost up the slope of life only to end in nothingness at the top, but the same process that carried it so far logically requires that it go on to perfection in the full and final realization of all its struggles and hopes and prophecies in the life immortal. This conclusion is required by the very rationality of the universe.

4. *Concepts of Philosophy*.

We now briefly refer to some of the fundamental concepts of philosophy which are basal in our modern views of the universe and bear on belief in immortality. As philosophy seeks to penetrate behind the proximate causes of science to final causes and ultimate reality, it cuts deeper into the substance of the world and the tissues of the soul than science and therefore bears more intimately upon our problem. Space permits only the barest suggestion of the basal concepts of this field of thought.

Though philosophy with its vast field may present at first an aspect of universal disagreement and confusion, yet it may be reduced for our purpose to four fundamental systems: agnosticism, materialism, pantheism, and personalism.

(1). Agnosticism affirms that it is impossible for us to know ultimate reality because we can perceive only phenomena or the outer appearances of the world and cannot penetrate through the veil into what lies behind; and it further affirms that the human mind in its very constitution is a fallacious organ of knowledge, as though it were a distorted lens that perverts all that is seen through it into false forms. The human mind is therefore incompetent to know anything as it is in itself, especially in the region of ultimate reality.

Agnosticism therefore writes "Unknowable" across the mystery of the universe and seals its lips as to any God or hope for us in this world. Faith in immortality finds no gleam of light in this system.

The answer to these claims is that in knowing phenomena, which are effects, we can know something of their cause; and the system is self-destructive, for if the human mind is an untrustworthy organ of knowledge, then it cannot know anything, not even that it cannot know, and all knowledge is at an end. We must trust the human mind as a competent organ of knowledge when critically used, or any and all knowledge is rendered impossible.

(2). The materialism that resolved mind into matter and the soul into a secretion of the brain is now hopelessly discredited and is gone from all the higher regions of thought. The impossibility of translating matter into mind remains and grows into a more impassable barrier. Matter itself has been dissolved in the alembic of science. It was first broken up into molecules and then these were divided into atoms which were long regarded as ultimate indivisible and indestructible particles that were supposed to remain rigid and immutable as the last limit and final frontier of matter.

But the atom itself has now been shown to be a highly complex system which is subject to violent disintegration into simpler elements. The atom of radium, as an example of several or of all atoms, is literally breaking up and expelling at great speed several streams of emanations, the débris of the exploding atom, the end-product and final residuum of this atomic disintegration of radium being lead.

All atoms are now known to be composed of electrons, which are particles very small as compared with the atom itself, and are bits of negative electricity revolving with a speed near that of light around a nucleus of positive electricity.

And what are electrons? They are believed to be

some modification of the universal ether variously described as "vortexes," "tensions," "strains," and "motions," in this medium. According to a theory recently propounded by Professor J. H. Jeans, a high English astronomical authority, the sun, along with all stars, in its fierce laboratory is transmuting electrons into light waves or energy and is thus radiating four million tons of its substance into space a second. If this theory is established, then matter and energy are proved to be identical. And what is the ether? We do not know, but it is declared to be "not matter,"[1] but a mysterious medium with very remarkable properties. Whatever it is, it acts as though it were pure force or undifferentiated energy, and is thus the very essence of the material universe.

Not only so, this ether acts as though it were a universal will working according to plan and purpose; and so it seems to be closely related to if not identical with the will of God! We are here on the very border between science and philosophy where the one steps into the other. Idealistic philosophers do not hesitate to take this step and affirm the essential spirituality of the material world, and some scientific thinkers do the same thing. Professor J. S. Haldane of the University of Birmingham, an eminent authority in the field of science, devotes an article in a recent number of *The Hibbert Journal* (April, 1923) to "the thesis that the material world which has been taken for a world of blind mechanism is in reality the spiritual world seen very partially and imperfectly, and that the only real world is the spiritual world."

[1] J. W. Nicholson, *Problems of Modern Science,* p. 30.

We do not press this point, but it is clear that matter as the basis of the old materialism has melted away into something very like spirit. As Mr. A. J. Balfour says, in his *Theism and Humanism*, "We know too much about matter to be materialists."

This at once frees the material world from the iron-bound mechanism of matter that left no possible room for mind, much less for immortal mind, and transmutes it into a roomy and friendly if not spiritual field for the earthly dwelling of the human soul and opens out infinite vistas for endless life in the world beyond.

(3). Pantheism merges the totality of existence in a universal ocean of impersonal being in which human souls are only evanescent bubbles that will presently burst and melt indistinguishably into this sea, leaving no perceptible trace behind. Immortality loses all personality and fades into unconscious existence.

This system contradicts our intuitive and ineradicable sense of personality and responsibility, which is our most certain knowledge.

(4). Personalism, whether dualistic or idealistic, finds spirit to be the ultimate reality and personality its highest expression, and thereby gives us a world in which God, the supreme Spirit, reigns, and finite created spirits have personality and responsibility in this world and hope of immortality in the next.

There are able agnostics, and many philosophers are pantheists in one or another of its many forms. The Orient is saturated and drugged with this powerful soporific. But the prevailing tendency of the human mind is towards some form of personalism. So strong is this tendency that even agnostics and pantheists may more or less unwittingly relapse into it. Mr. Herbert Spencer admitted that his Unknowable Power is "probably," "psychical" and "hyperpersonal," that is spiritual and personal, and pantheism even in the Orient breaks, among the unthinking multitudes, into myriads of personal gods, and, among the more thoughtful, slips into various personalistic forms.

The great thinkers from Plato to Kant and Descartes and Leibnitz and on down to Bowne and Royce in our country have been personalistic in their philosophy, and though there are notable exceptions, yet this is the prevailing philosophy of our day.[2]

Modern science and philosophy, then, do not uproot the hope of immortality, but offer it a friendly soil and congenial atmosphere in which to grow.

5. *Analogies in Nature.*

Are there any hints and hopes or analogies of immortal life in nature itself? At first glance it might seem to be one universal unbroken tomb in which all life at

[2] As an illustration of this we may cite a recent comprehensive and solid work on philosophy entitled *Man and the Cosmos*, by Joseph A. Leighton, Professor of Philosophy in Ohio State University. Professor Leighton, who denominates his system "Dynamic Idealism," states his fundamental conclusion as follows: "If there be no personal or superpersonal ground for their lives, the meaning and goal of nature's evolution and humanity's ceaseless travail seems to turn to nothingness. Therefore faith in the spiritual character or selfhood of the supreme unity is involved in the recognition that personal values are the finest fruits of the process of reality. Such faith is rational, since without it the whole process of reality, with all its striving and suffering, all its passion and visions, all its achievements and heroisms, turns to dust and ashes." P. 497.

death is forever "sealed in iron hills." But, as usual, a deeper look discloses some analogies that afford suggestions and gleams of hope that are not without value.

Life breaks into myriad forms and fulfills itself often in strange and startling ways. It spins its fine thread in unbroken continuity through all ages and across all chasms; and it passes through many wonderful transformations and resurrections that suggest similar and deeper possibilities in human life.

Life in all its higher forms passes through a kind of death and resurrection as it is packed away in a seed or cell and then bursts into new glory. A seed drops into the soil and perishes, but it transmits its life to a new growth and springs up in a stalk and breaks into bloom and renews its life. Every winter buries vegetable life in a grave, which in the spring rises in a glorious resurrection. The same process in the higher animals takes place in the womb in which life retreats into the embryo and becomes a mere thread of cells and then buds anew into all the strength and beauty of youthful life.

The primal thread of life propagates itself without break. The simplest form of life in single-celled plants and animals multiplies by division. A single cell divides into two, and this process continues without end, and thus in this line of descent there is no process of old age, degeneration and death, but the vital thread spins itself unbroken and unspent through ever-renewed youth and deathless life. The individuals of such a species existing to-day are simply the infinitely divided cells that originated far back in the geological morning when the first pulse of life beat on the planet. They are older than any existing mountains and continents and they will continue in unbroken lines until the last pulse of life throbs on the earth.

But a similar continuous thread of germplasm runs through all the forms of life, and the individuals in the world to-day, of all species including man, have budded out on this continuous scarlet thread and are thus connected by a kind of immortality with their first ancestors and will hand on this inextinguishable torch of deathless life to their last descendants.

Alternate generation presents wonderful facts which are strangely significant. Many of the lower plants and animals exist in one form in one generation and in the next generation in a wholly different form. The first form may be a free animal living in an external medium, and the second may be a parasite passing its entire existence within another animal, to be set free again in the next alternate generation. In many instances these alternate forms were long supposed to be independent species until their strange connection was discovered. The first form seems to have perished, but its life is continued in another form and in another environment or world.

Stranger and more significant still is the phenomenon of metamorphosis. An animal begins its existence in one form and then suddenly changes into another that may bear no resemblance in organs and functions, appearance and activity, medium and mode of life to the first form. Familiar instances are the transformation of a tadpole into a frog and of a caterpillar into a butterfly. The caterpillar is a shaggy, slow-moving creature, repulsive in appearance. It lives without change for a period and then passes into a quiescent pupa state in which a wonderful process rapidly takes place. The whole structure of the worm is torn down and reduced, in Fabre's phrase, to "a thick soup" and rebuilt into a new creature, which then emerges as a swift-winged, gorgeously painted and splendidly bejeweled butterfly that flits and flashes about as a living flower in the wide free world of the atmosphere. The insect world is full of these metamorphoses that are among the greatest marvels and mysteries of life.

If life finds so many ways of escaping from one form to another and of slipping through the dark gates of apparent death into new youth and larger worlds, will not the higher and more permanent and precious form of human life pass through the transition of earthly death and emerge in more glorious forms in a fairer world? Shall the microbe be older than the rock-ribbed mountains and still be fresh with immortal youth, and yet the thread of the human soul be snapped after a few brief years? Shall the lowly worm become the fairy butterfly, passing from one world to another, and yet man be denied this power and privilege?

All life is teleologic. It is forward-looking and moves toward an end. And its end may be out of sight in a distant and different world. Often we can see it moving from the lower to the higher and from darkness to light, from bondage to liberty, from a narrow shut-in womb to a wide free world, from seed to flower and from egg to song, from the unborn babe to the poet and philosopher, and, by the projection of this analogy and law of life, from this mortal human life to the life immortal and from earth to heaven.

We should not put too much weight on these analogies. They will seem fanciful and even false to some; and we do not claim that they are all analogies in the deepest sense of identity. But they are at the least suggestive parables of nature. We do not suspend our faith and argument mainly on these suggestive facts, but we may weave them as strands into our many-sided meditation on this mystery and hope. Nature is often prophetic and is hinting at deep laws and great possibilities for us, and we do well to place our ear close to its bosom and try to catch every beat of its heart and every whisper of its voice.

> If the red slayer thinks he slays,
>   Or if the slain thinks he is slain,
> They know not well the subtle ways
>   I keep, and pass, and turn again.
> —*Emerson.*

The Last Adventure

Gleams hint that life upon some future waits;
  The worm cannot forecast the butterfly—
And yet the transformation but creates
A step in the same Nature which now mates
  Our own—and may life's mystery untie.

Mayhap the butterfly this message brings:—
  "The law, uncomprehended, I obey;
Although the lowliest of earth-bred things,
Even I have been reborn with urgent wings,
  And heavenward fly—who crept but yesterday."

In life's fair mansion I am but a guest;
  And life will bring fulfillment of the gleam.
I trust this last adventure is the best,
The crowning of this earthly life's behest,
  The consummation of the poet's dream.
        —*James Terry White.*

47

CHAPTER III

THE MOST POWERFUL OBJECTION
TO IMMORTALITY

Let us grapple at once with the most powerful objection to human immortality that if possible we may break its force and clear it out of the way for positive considerations.

1. *Dependence of the Soul on the Body.*

This objection is the dependence of the soul on the body and its apparent dissipation with the dissolution of the body in death. The mutual relation of the soul and body is one of the most elusive and difficult problems of psychology and metaphysics, though the fact is plain and is attested in our constant experience that this relation is some kind of interaction.

The body and the soul develop together and keep pace with each other at every point and step. Every mental state or action is accompanied with a corresponding physical action, and every physical change in the body induces a corresponding change in the mind. A diseased spot in the brain may produce paralysis and convulsions, or mental depression and insanity, and the removal of the diseased area by surgery may cause a complete cure. The soul is exquisitely sensitive to changes in the body and goes up or down with its condition. As the body

48

fails in old age, the soul generally declines with it and sometimes becomes only a vestige or reminiscence of its former self. And in death the same crisis that stills the heart also seems to extinguish consciousness and obliterate the soul forever. In short, we know the soul only in connection with the body, and the two seem to come into existence and to perish together.

This objection appears powerful and gives us a pause and undoubtedly is the greatest hindrance in the way of believing in immortality, especially among scientific men. Yet reflection begins to call forth considerations that blunt its force. It is at once seen that this argument is based upon our ignorance of a disembodied state, and we cannot rest an argument upon mere ignorance, for our experience is limited to a narrow field in this world and there must be secrets in the vast mystery of existence of which we have never dreamed.

2. *The Body as a Means to the Soul.*

There are grounds for thinking that the body is a means to the soul from which the soul can disengage itself. In fact the soul is continually shedding the body as its dead cells and waste products are flowing away from it in a steady stream and being constantly replaced, so that the body is perpetually dying and casting its own corpse into the grave of nature and is recreated and resurrected as a new body many times in the course of life. If the soul can thus continually disengage itself from the body in life, may it not finally divorce itself from the flesh in death?

The great fear at this point has been that the soul may be shown to be a mere form of molecular motion in the body. But the old materialism that secreted thought from the brain as bile from the liver is, as we have seen, discredited. There is no possibility of passing, as Tyndall, himself close to being a materialist, long ago said, from the physics of the brain to the consciousness of the mind. The brain as a material organ is subject to the laws of matter, including the conservation of its energy. But no unit of physical energy in passing through the brain disappears and is transformed into its equivalent in thought; and no thought of the mind is converted into any kind of physical energy. There is some kind of interaction between these two forms of reality, but it is not that of transformation by which one of these kinds passes into the other, as when electricity is converted into heat and heat into chemical affinity. Mind and body are mysteriously linked together, and yet they are disparate and never transfused.[1]

3. *The Architectonic Power of Mind.*

But we now come to a deeper truth at this point. As Kant wrought the Copernican revolution of reversing the relation of matter to mind, so a similar revolution has been accomplished in the relation of body and soul. Life was formerly regarded as a product of the body, but now we are coming to see that the body is a product of life. Life molds the body to its own shape and use in all its myriad forms from single-celled plants and animals up to the highest life in man. In every seed and germ cell an invisible architect is at work building an appro-

[1] For recent able discussions of this problem see Professor J. B. Pratt's *Matter and Spirit* and Professor William McDougall's *Body and Mind*.

priate tabernacle for its tenant, and this architect is life.

Let Huxley, with his marvelous insight and skill, show us this architect at work. "The student of nature," he says in his *Lay Sermons,* "wonders the more and is astonished the less, the more conversant he becomes with her operations; but of all the perennial miracles she offers to his inspection, perhaps the most worthy of admiration is the development of a plant or animal from the embryo. Examine the recently laid egg of some common animal, such as a salamander or a newt. It is a minute spheroid in which the best microscope will reveal nothing but a structureless sac, inclosing a glairy fluid, holding granules in suspension. But strange possibilities lie dormant in that semifluid globule. Let a moderate supply of warmth reach its watery cradle, and the plastic matter undergoes changes so rapid and yet so steady and purposelike in their succession, that one can only compare them to those operated by a skilled modeler upon a formless lump of clay. As with an invisible trowel, the mass is divided and subdivided into smaller and smaller portions, until it is reduced to an aggregation of granules not too large to build withal the finest fabrics of the nascent organism. And, then, it is as if a delicate finger traced out the line to be occupied by the spinal column, and molded the contour of the body; pinching up the head at one end, the tail at the other, and fashioning flank and limb into due salamandrine proportions, in so artistic a way, that, after watching the process hour by hour, one is almost involuntarily possessed by the notion, that some more subtle aid to vision than an achromatic, would show the hidden artist, with his plan before him, striving with skillful manipulation to perfect his work."

If this wonderful architectonic and teleological description applies to the lowly animal, how much more aptly does it apply to man. With equal anatomic knowledge and literary skill of description Dr. William Hanna Thompson, in his *Brain and Personality* and again in his *Life, Death and Immortality,* lays open the chamber of the human brain and shows us the architect of life at work. The brain is at first a soft pulpy mass, which instinct and habit and purpose begin to mold and carve into shape and use. All is wrought out according to plan and specifications. Centers of nerve cells are first roughly blocked out and then more finely shaped and finished, and a complex network of filaments is spun from center to center, weaving the whole organ into a marvelously intricate and exquisite mechanism, quick to catch the faintest whisper of breath or stand the strain and stress of the most violent storm from the external world. Each sense, such as the eye and the ear, has its own center, and every kind of action constructs its own special receiver and transmitter, as a receiver in a wireless station or radio is tuned to its own peculiar waves.

Language, for example, has its own center, which by the conscious efforts of the mind in learning language is slowly shaped and tuned to that speech. When a new language is acquired, as when one whose native tongue is English learns French, a new layer of French-receiving cells is built over the old layer of English-receiving cells, so that the mind for this new use carves a new shape out of the block of the brain. And so the process goes on through the whole body throughout all life, although as life advances in years the brain grows less plastic and more refractory and set in its ways.

Life thus molds the body and is not its product. The soul is the unseen architect of the body, the tenant that builds its own wondrous temple. The brain does not make the mind so much as the mind makes the brain. "Form," maintains a recent authoritative biologist (E. S. Russell in *Form and Function*), "is a manifestation of function; the essence of life is activity, not organization."

In the volume of essays entitled *Immortality*, edited by B. H. Streeter, the chapter on "The Mind and the Brain" is by James Arthur Hadfield, Surgeon in the Royal Navy. He says in the introduction to his chapter: "I propose to bring forward evidence which will encourage us in the belief that in the course of evolution the mind shows an ever-increasing tendency to free itself from physical control and, breaking loose from its bonds, to assert its independence and live a life undetermined except by the laws of its own nature. The main argument of this essay is that the tendency of the mind towards independence and autonomy suggests the possibility of its becoming entirely liberated from the body, and continuing to live disembodied and free." The chapter adduces cumulative evidence along this line.

"Physicians," Dr. Thompson says, "were once charged with being the most materialistic of all professional men, but they are now coming forward with discoveries about the unseen personality in us, which furnish the most conclusive arguments against the doctrines of materialism."

4. *The Body as the Inlet of the Soul.*

Professor William James, who was both an anatomist and a psychologist and thus stood close to the two most difficult fields of fact to harmonize with belief in immortality, in his Harvard Ingersoll Lecture on *Human Immortality* propounded an original view of the relation of the body to the soul. He says that the body may be viewed as either the productive or the transmissive cause of the soul. In the former case, consciousness is a light burning in the brain and kindled by the brain; in the latter case, the brain is a window letting in the light from the outside. According to this latter view the body is immersed in a cosmic sea of light or intelligence which filters in through the transparent cortex of the brain and is the light that lighteth every man. If this suggests that this light of personal consciousness will be dissipated and reabsorbed in the general sea of consciousness at the dissolution of the body, Professor James thought that it would acquire sufficient steadiness and fixity to retain personal consciousness permanently, so that each one after death will be able to say, "I am the same personal being who in old time upon earth had those experiences."

A similar view, held by some psychologists and theologians, is that the subconscious or subliminal self is the inlet through which the general sea of consciousness, or the life of God, pours into the body and forms the soul, and that this landlocked harbor or bay of human consciousness will endure in personal form after the barrier of the body is swept away in death.

However speculative these views may be, they serve to show that in the judgment of scientific thinkers the relation of the body to the mind is not that of physical cause and effect, but rather that the body is only a temporary means of the soul and a hindrance to its fuller life which it shall enter upon when it is set free from the bonds of earth and launches out upon the deep of the eternal world.

5. *The Power of the Soul over the Body.*

The body bears all the marks of being the instrument or tool of the soul. The soul sharply distinguishes itself from the body, handles it, resists it, and especially does it master and mold it to its own use. The whole system of muscles and nerves becomes an extension of the will to do its bidding. The will has the mysterious power of releasing currents of energy in the brain that leap out through the nerves and muscles into the world and pierce mountains and carve continents and finally impinge on the frontiers of the universe. Feelings paint themselves on the face, flushing it red or blanching it white. At times the soul overpowers the body and strikes through its flesh with crushing force. Knowing how the mind under a great stroke of sorrow may blast and wither the body in a single night and how great joy may rejuvenate it, we are prepared for startling facts in this field. The "stigmata" of the saints, in which the mind burnt right through the body or stabbed and slashed it as with a sword, are supported by weighty evidence. Disease comes or goes at the bidding of the mind. No doubt excessive claims have been made for the curative power of the mind in disease, but that it is a vital factor in the matter is emphasized by medical authorities and is receiving increased attention in all quarters.

As life advances, the body loses its strength and suppleness, its responsiveness to the demands of the soul, and becomes stiff and refractory, inefficient and impotent. It degenerates into a worn-out machine, a blunted or broken tool. This crippled condition of the body is an adequate explanation of the impaired mental powers in old age. May not the tool become broken or worn-out and be laid aside without impairing the skill of the worker?

When a telegraph instrument stops working the operator does not stop thinking. The first cable laid under the Atlantic after operating a short time suddenly ceased to transmit messages. The operators in America did not conclude that the operators in Europe had ceased to exist when that wire stopped working: they only concluded that something was wrong with the wire. So we are not to conclude that the soul has ceased to exist when it ceases to communicate through the body; the body may be simply worn out or broken and the soul may be using some other vehicle of expression. As we know that the telegraph instrument cannot come into existence apart from the operator, but that the operator can exist apart from the instrument, so we know the brain cannot exist apart from the mind, but we may infer and have strong reasons for thinking that the mind can exist apart from the brain.

The soul is less and less dependent on the body as it develops its own inner resources. It starts in utter bondage to the body, literally sunk in the flesh. But as it develops it outstrips the body, and the soul rises above sense, and the spirit above the flesh. More and more, as life advances, the soul becomes self-dependent and dominant, loosed from servitude to the body and endowed with internal resources. In some instances, when the body has shrunk and withered almost to the vanishing point, the soul flames out in the greatest intensity and power. It looks as though the soul were gradually outgrowing the body and letting go of this crutch, while it is developing wings on which to soar into a wider and freer life.

6. *Is the Soul Ever Disembodied?*

One of the difficulties of faith in immortality is the impossibility of conceiving the soul without a body and the instinctive fear we have of such a state. We know life only in the body and are frightened at the idea of a ghost and do not want to be one.

But this notion assumes that the human soul at death passes into a disembodied state, and we do not know and need not think that this is the fact. The body is a marvelous mechanism, the costly product of countless ages of toil in the process of evolution, and it is necessary to our life in this world. Let us not think it is an unessential or unimportant appendage to the soul that may lightly be cast aside. May we not rather infer that in the next stage of existence the soul will be furnished with an appropriate body, or that it will weave around itself a garment and fashion an instrument that will suit its needs in its wider and richer life there, even as its fleshly body has served it here?

The present body may be only a temporary tent or hut for the soul while its proper palace is being built. "Any continuity of life," says Dr. James Ward in *The Realm of Ends*, "with no continuity of either organism or environment seems quite inconceivable. But there is nothing in our present knowledge to show that there cannot be any other mode of embodiment than that with which we are here familiar." And he ventures the suggestion: "It may be that in the course of this life the nervous system, by its ultimate habitudes, should form a finer organization, and that this in the moment and act of death should be disentangled from the coarser frame."

This is the Christian faith. Paul viewed the present body as an "earthly tabernacle" and contrasted it with "an house not made with hands, eternal in the heavens." "It is sown in corruption; it is raised in incorruption: it is sown in dishonor; it is raised in glory: it is sown in weakness; it is raised in power; it is sown a natural body; it is raised a spiritual body." The soul at death may cast away "this muddy vesture of decay," because it has become an outworn garment, in order that it may weave around itself a closelier fitting, more supple and serviceable, and more splendid and beautiful robe of life in the eternal world.

> So is myself withdrawn into my depths,
> The soul retreated from the perished brain,
> Whence it was wont to feel and use the world
> Through these dull members, done with long ago.
> Yet I myself remain; I feel myself:
> And there is nothing lost. Let be, awhile!
> —*Browning.*

CHAPTER IV

NATURAL GROUNDS OF BELIEF
IN IMMORTALITY

We are now passing from the negative to the positive side of our problem, from difficulties and doubts to intimations and proofs. While we must brood over the subject and let it call forth every suggestion and while it is largely atmospheric and grows best in the mystic mood of meditation, yet it also is ready to face concrete facts and connect arguments with the links of logic.

We begin our investigation as close to ourselves as possible, down on the bedrock of personal experience, as the astronomer, when about to cast his measuring line out among the stars, takes his stand on the ground under his feet.

1. *The Soul as Reality in Itself.*

The first bit of reality we indubitably know is our own soul or self or consciousness. We know this by immediate awareness or intuition. External objects are known to us through the mediation of the senses, which are of the nature of colored lenses that impose the secondary or sensational qualities of matter upon these objects and thereby give them their sensational appearances. A change in the senses, as in the retina of the eye or the tympanum of the ear, would thereby effect a change in the sensational nature or appearance of the object and might even transform it profoundly. Sense perception thus gives us knowledge of reality at second-hand, or knowledge that has passed through a process of transmission and transformation.

Not so with our knowledge of the self. We look into our consciousness, not through senses, but directly without any transmitting or transforming medium. We are immediately aware of the self, of its states and activities, and there is no room for perversion or error in a process of transmission. The self is at once subject and object of consciousness with nothing interposed between them, like the senses, to dim or blur the vision. Consciousness is self-consciousness, the knowing subject and the known object are identical in one and the same self.

Such knowledge is the surest and clearest we can have. Its stream is not mixed and muddied with the sediment of the senses, or distorted with their transforming processes, but is direct vision and pure light. We thus know ourselves better than we know anything else.

Here is our first knowledge of reality. It is not knowledge of a phenomenon, as is our knowledge of the external world which consists of appearances or symbolic representations of things, but our self-consciousness is knowledge of the noumenon, of immediate reality or the thing in itself. We thus have in our own selfhood a bit of ultimate reality, and this leads us strongly towards the conclusion that we have in the soul a sample of all reality, one of the tiny bricks of which the universe is built. While philosophy may be searching for ultimate reality far off in the heaven above and in the earth beneath, we may find it right at home, for it is nigh us, even in our heart.

Idealistic philosophy assimilates all reality with spirit, discerns in matter a manifestation of mind, finds physical forces to be living energies, and resolves the whole universe, with the signal exception of finite spirits, into the activity of the Infinite Spirit, or God. Whatever may be our view at this point, we must admit that the soul is a dynamic agent or living energy. It would be absurd to grant to chemical affinity or gravitation a degree of reality which we deny to the active and imperial human soul.

2. *The Conservation of Reality.*

To this dynamic agent the principle of the conservation of energy must now apply. This principle is one of the established doctrines of modern science. The manifold forms of energy we see manifested in the physical world are all mutually equivalent and interchangeable and are being constantly transformed into one another, but are never increased, diminished, or annihilated. Motion becomes heat, heat becomes electricity, electricity becomes chemical affinity, chemical affinity becomes light, and light becomes motion, and thus the Protean circuit runs its endless round. Matter itself, as we have seen, may be interchangeable with energy.

But at no point in this process does an infinitesimal atom of energy drop out of the circuit and vanish into nothingness. Experiment always finds the transformed energy exactly equal to the original, and any deficiency or excess in the resulting product would be unthinkable. The mind cannot find or conceive any point in the process where any minutest unit of energy could lapse. Thus the sum total of energy in the physical universe remains a constant quantity so far as our science and philosophy can discover.

The meaning of this infinitely-interlaced, exquisitely-balanced, self-perpetuating system of physical energies, according to philosophical conception, is that the divine activities are a unified system in which any change at one point is attended with a compensating or corresponding change at other points. A divine act or thought can never perish, but abides in the eternal life of God.

The same principle now applies to the human soul. As it is a center and agent of mental activity, a finite copy of God's infinite Spirit, it can change the form and direction of its activities, but its energies themselves can never cease, its spiritual energy can never be spent and vanish. It is a bit of the immortal energy of God and can never die.

There is no escape from this conclusion unless we annul the principle of the conservation of energy, which is one of the most solidly established principles of our modern scientific thought. And this law applies to the soul even though we hold that the physical energy of matter and the spiritual energy of the soul are of a different nature; for we can no more think of spiritual reality than we can of physical reality lapsing into nothingness. We have thus at this point hitched our wagon to one of the most splendid stars of science.

But, it may be said, this law only assures the perpetuity of the spiritual principle or energy of the soul, but not its personality. The soul is immortal in its essence, but it melts back into the infinite Spirit whence it came, as raindrops, having been distilled out of the sea, fall back into its depths. This is a powerful objection to personal immortality, and it will next be considered.

3. *Personality: Its Nature, Worth and Power.*

We now note the fact, of immense significance in this argument, that the soul, which is the first piece of reality we indubitably know, is personal spirit, or is constituted as a personality. Personality is consciousness consisting of perceptive and reflective thought, sensibility and responsible will. We think, we feel, we will, we do these three things and we never can do more or less. In our consciousness we are always thinking and feeling and willing simultaneously. Any one of these modes may at any moment be predominant and seem to submerge the others, but the three are always acting together, though in varying degrees and combinations.

The intellect mirrors the world in sense perception and reconstructs it in thought, draws conclusions in reasoning, sees visions in imagination and constructs purposes and plans. Feeling suffuses the ideas of the mind with general excitement and imparts to them their interest and worth and pours a stream of motive energy upon the will. The will is the self-control of the soul by which it chooses its own ends and motives and concentrates its energy into imperial power over life and nature. All these faculties and activities constitute a unitary organism in which the whole enters into each operation and which in its totality is characterized by growth, habit, law, liberty, purpose and responsibility.

Yet this unity diverges into variety and deep distinctions. It has a varied and rich capacity of perceiving and feeling and acting on different kinds or aspects of the infinite manifold of reality. When acting on objects in their intellectual nature it has knowledge; in their esthetic nature, a sense of beauty; in their ethical nature, a sense of duty; and when acting on objects in their relations to God it is exercising its sense of worship and experiencing religion.

Personality is the supreme worth of our human world. It is a great stride forward in the process of evolution and creation, an abrupt break and difference in kind from all that went before. It can be explained only on Bateson's principle of "a variation in which something has been added." [1]

All theories of his rank admit that man stands at the top of the creation, the highest and finest product of evolution. His erect form and upward-looking face distinguish him among animals, and his whole physical organization, brain capacity, and mental power lift him out of their class. His moral and spiritual nature elevates him still higher, and he alone among creatures known to us is crowned with full-orbed, imperial personality.

This is indeed a crown that gives him sovereignty and a scepter over creation. He captures and trains into nimble servants all the forces of nature and subdues the earth and turns its wilderness into cultivated fields and splendid cities. His soul secretes civilization, and the whole vast material structure of our human world is simply the outgrowth and extension of his own personality.

In his science man reveals the rank of personality as he reaches immeasurably beyond his hands and even his

[1] Page 37.

eyes into the world as it recedes into the infinitely small and stretches away into the infinitely great. Through his microscope he peers down towards atoms and electrons, and through his telescope he gazes out through boundless spaces. Standing on this tiny earth he throws his net out into the star-sprinkled splendor of the night and catches suns and systems, sifts them through his fingers, and analyzes them into their elements. By means of his spectroscope he splits the light of sun and stars into its components and makes them tell the story of their substance, distance and speed, and even seizes the nebulæ, filling vast spaces with their filmy matter and faint light, and drags them into his laboratory and crushes them into his crucible and extorts from them the secret of their constitution.

He turns up the rocky leaves of the globe and reads in their hieroglyphics the history of a hundred million years. He glances backward through illimitable vistas and sees nebulæ condensing into solar systems and suns, and forward through far-stretching æons and sees them cooling until their fires are extinguished and they are shrouded in snow and coffined in ice. He grasps the universe in its grand law-saturated totality in which no atom ever gets out of place and no star ever shoots a forbidden ray.

He relates the near to the far and the small to the great in one organism of interworking unity and exquisite sympathy from molecule to mountain and from gnat to Zodiac. He sees that every star lends a friendly ray to the rose and would not dare deny that the fragrant breath of the rose is grateful to the constellations. He knows, with Mrs. Browning, that

THE CHRISTIAN BELIEF IN IMMORTALITY

No lily-muffled hum of summer bee,
But finds some coupling with the spinning stars;
No pebble at your feet but proves a sphere;
No chaffinch but implies the cherubim.

And yet man's science, while more spectacular, is of subordinate value to his art and ethics, sociology and politics, education and religion. His soul blossoms out into the glorious products of his poetry and painting, sculpture and architecture and music. He builds governments and dreams of a parliament of man. He studies social problems and perils, feels the sorrows of society, and strives to plan and construct a social order that will give every human being the opportunity and means of a decent and worthy and beautiful life. He climbs the stairway of philosophy to catch a glimpse of the Ultimate Reality, and in religion rises to his highest and best as he sees and serves the one true and living God.

Character that is true and pure, good and beautiful and blessed, has value above every other possession and power and is the supreme worth and final end to which all other things are means. This is the diamond that scratches every other stone, the inner worth that outranks and outshines all outer wealth. And character is found only in personality.

Personality is power. It is the master force of human civilization, without which coal and iron and steam and electricity could not forge a beam or build a hut. It is this power that constructs the whole material fabric of our civilization and makes the great statesman, orator, thinker, poet, preacher, artist, or leader in any field. It was by the force of his personality that Demosthenes swayed Athens, Cæsar mastered Rome, Paul drove the wedge of the gospel into Europe, Luther created the Reformation, Napoleon dominated the kings of his day, and Lincoln liberated a fettered race. It was the personality of Columbus that, amidst the fears and appeals and threats of his cowardly sailors as they cried out against the terrors of the unknown sea, held the prow of his vessel ever westward, every morning keeping it in the track of the sun and every evening driving it deeper into the dark. It is personality that makes great discoveries, writes great books, paints great pictures, dreams great buildings, achieves triumphs and heroisms, and carves names high on the pillar of fame. Almost every great historic achievement or institution is the lengthened shadow of some supreme personality.

Personalities are the mountain peaks that mark the culminating points in the range of events and lift the level of their region. And yet even the greatest personality and most splendid genius only discloses and pushes into prominence the worth that is at least lying latent in the humblest human being and even in the little child.

In our human world all things are interpreted in terms of and derive their worth from personality. Soil and shower and sunshine, mineral and vegetable and all the physical energies of nature have their value determined by their availability for human use. The reason an acre of ground in Europe or America is worth so much more than one in Central Africa is to be found in the human persons that live on it. Take all the people out of a rich and splendid city like New York or London and its value would instantly vanish and become one with Nineveh and Tyre. Nothing in our human world has any worth until it is related to human use. Man's presence must be indicated in the wildest waste to give interest even to a painting.

More and more our civilization is exalting the worth of human personality from the top to the bottom of society. It is this sense of the supreme value of personality that has struck the fetters from the slave, elevated woman, and is throwing protection around the child. The worth of simple personality is being raised above ancient rights of property. It is this that brought thrones and crowns crashing down in the Great War, in which democracy asserted itself against autocracy, and personality against brute power. It is this that is dissolving and leveling special privileges and social distinctions of royalty and nobility and wealth and is flooding the world with democracy. It is this that is ringing out false pride of place and blood and ringing in the common love of good; that is ringing in the valiant man and free, the larger heart, the kindlier hand; ringing out the thousand wars of old and ringing in the thousand years of peace; ringing out the darkness of the land and ringing in the Christ that is to be.

And so all things in our human world converge and climax in the supreme rank and worth of human personality. Take man off the earth and it would fall to the level of a dead world such as we see in the moon, and even below this, for the moon has value as it is related to man. Of course earth and moon and all the worlds must have some worth other than that due to man, but such value must be derived from their relations to some other persons or Person, for viewed simply as material globes their whole value vanishes.

Personality is the only adequate final explanation of

68

the universe. We immediately know order and plan and energy only in our own intelligence and will, and then we proceed to extend and apply these inner principles to outer things. We look upon human behavior as it goes on in business, society, politics, art, literature, religion, upon the whole swarming ant-hill of our human world, and we infer in these moving bodies the presence and activity of souls like our own. The entire human spectacle is meaningless until we thus interpret it, and personality instantly lights it up with this inner power and explanation.

An extension of the same principle puts intelligence and will behind and within all the appearances and activities of the universe as its inner reason and energy. We can really understand these activities only when we interpret their order and plan as the work of intelligence and their energies as the exertion of will. The universe, like our human world, is rationally understood only as we construe it in terms of personality; and then personality becomes our ultimate explanation which cannot be explained and must be accepted as at once the initial and the final fact of existence, the Alpha and Omega, the beginning and the end, the final Mystery that gathers into itself and explains all other mysteries and in which we rest.

4. *The Permanence of Personality.*

Personality, being the highest product and final crown of life and of the universe, must be permanent, or all value vanishes with it.

Its permanence is seen in its persistence through all earthly vicissitudes. While it develops from germinal consciousness to fullblown power, yet after emerging into selfhood it retains its central core of consciousness, which does not change with the years but remains as the identical self. Its outward circumstances are in a state of ceaseless flux and at times pass through tremendous shocks and upheavals; its very body flows away from it in a steady stream and is constantly replaced with new tissues; its subjective experience is in a state of incessant change and development, and at intervals encounters catastrophic crises and is swept by terrible storms; and yet none of these things rolls it from its base, but its central self persists as the same personality. The pathological condition of divided and multiple personality, strange as it often is, does not invalidate this general normal fact, a point that will be considered later in this study.

If personality can survive such constant and deep changes and even repeatedly put off the entire body and clothe itself in a new garment of flesh, will it not survive the still greater shock of death and weave around itself a new body adapted to its new condition?

This conclusion has been accepted and asserted by some of our ablest scientific thinkers, the class of men that find it most difficult to adopt such views. "What we are claiming," says Sir Oliver Lodge in his *Science and Immortality*, "is no less than this—that, whereas it is certain that the present body cannot long exist without the soul, it is quite possible and indeed necessary for the soul to exist without the body. We base this claim on the soul's manifest transcendence, on its genuine reality, and on the general law of the persistence of real existence. . . . Immortality is the persistence of the essential and the real; it applies to things which the universe has gained—things which, once acquired, cannot be let go."

The view of John Fiske, as set forth in his *Destiny of Man*, is also of special interest and weight: "Now the more thoroughly we comprehend that process of evolution by which things have come to be what they are, the more we are likely to feel that to deny the everlasting spiritual element in Man is to rob the whole process of meaning. It goes far toward putting us to permanent intellectual confusion, and I do not see that any one has as yet alleged, or is ever likely to allege, a sufficient reason for our accepting so dire a conclusion. . . . The greatest philosopher of modern times, the master and teacher of all who shall study the processes of evolution for many a day to come, holds that the conscious soul is not the product of a collocation of material particles, but is in the deepest sense a divine effluence. According to Mr. Spencer, the divine energy which is manifested throughout the knowable universe is the same energy that wells up in consciousness. Speaking for myself, I can see no insuperable difficulty in the notion that at some period in the evolution of Humanity this divine spark may have acquired sufficient concentration and steadiness to survive the wreck of material forms and endure forever. Such a crowning wonder seems to me no more than the fit climax to a creative work that has been ineffably beautiful and marvelous in all its myriad stages."

Even Mr. Darwin made the significant confession: "Believing, as I do, that man in the distant future will be a far more perfect creature than he now is, it is an

71

intolerable thought that he and all other sentient beings are doomed to complete annihilation after such long-continued slow progress. To those who fully admit the immortality of the human soul, the destruction of one world will not appear so dreadful."

These views of eminent evolutionists introduce and throw light upon the question which we have already touched upon, What effect does the theory of evolution have upon the hope of immortality? The popular impression appears to be that its effect is unfavorable if not fatal. The theory seems to suggest that all things come by a slow irresistible process of development, and bloom and ripen on the vast mystic tree of life, and then inevitably drop and perish in the general stream of nature; and the depressing thought is borne in upon us, at times with fearful force, that the human soul is only the topmost and finest blossom on the tree and withers and falls as any common leaf.

This view is graphically expressed in a powerful passage in Bertrand Russell's *Philosophical Essays* in which he declares that "all the labors of the ages, all the devotion, all the inspiration, all the noonday brightness of human genius, are destined to extinction in the vast death of the solar system, and the whole temple of Man's achievement must inevitably be buried beneath the débris of a universe in ruins."

The frightfulness of the picture must not keep us from facing and accepting it if it is true, but many roads lead us away from such a dreadful precipice plunging into the corpse-trench of the universe. The doctrine of evolution, on which this pessimistic view is largely based, is only a descriptive account of the successions of the phenomenal world and leaves untouched the causal power that underlies them; and this causal power, theistic philosophy holds, is the immanent intelligence and will of God, who is energizing in the world and producing all its activities and its whole development in the order of his plan and purpose. This resolves evolution into a process of the spiritual world in which souls have their congenial home and sets it in a friendly attitude towards this hope.

But there is still further confirmation of this hope in the theory. Evolution throughout its whole course is a process of producing ends which then enter as means upon a higher stage of development. The atom appears to be the product of one incomprehensibly long period of evolution; but it was no sooner produced than it was taken up into higher combinations in molecules and chemical compounds.

This inorganic matter was then transmuted into organized forms of life, and throughout this long climb we see the same principle at every stage and step. The mineral is food for the vegetable, the vegetable for the animal, and the animal for man. The wheat stalk, having ripened the wheat, perishes, but the grain is gathered into the granary. The apple, having grown upon the tree, is detached from its stem and passes into higher life. The end of each stage of evolution marks a critical point where the product is cut off from the process and raised to a higher level.

The direction in which this principle points is plain: it points to a higher life for man. His soul ripens on the stem of the body and then is detached and the body perishes. But the whole analogy of evolution requires ted that there may be an invasion of the nervous system of one person by another personality. Dr. Mitchell finds that the phenomena of hypnotic personalities, mediumistic personalities and multiple personalities are in some degree interrelated and interwoven, and that the separating of these tangled skeins of personality is one of the problems of the future.

As bearing on the doctrine of immortality, however, Dr. Mitchell holds that we shall be driven to some unitary soul in order to account for all the phenomena observed. "One unitary soul," he concludes, "may persist behind all dissociations of consciousness, but it will be unable to appear as a unity and its manifestations may be fragmentary and discordant. Its unity will be masked by the imperfection of its instrument." This "underlying unity" is the essential fact in the argument, at this point, for the immortality of the soul. Pathological conditions are never a sound basis for conclusions that relate to normal states, and it is the normal and healthy and not the abnormal and diseased brain that affords ground for our belief in the permanence of the human soul through all its vicissitudes, however strange and mysterious they may be.

6. *The Special Worth of Great Souls.*

The course of this argument applies to all human souls as beings of essential worth; but it impresses us most vividly and profoundly in the case of extraordinary souls.

Greatness brings out inner principles in accumulated power. We can scarcely measure gravitation in a mere mote floating in the air or in a molecule, but it becomes tremendous in the pressure of a mountain on its base, or in the pull of the moon or the sun on the earth; and we can see more of the sun's splendor reflected in a diamond than in a common bit of glass or a pebble. Life seems of small worth in a microbe, but it mounts up into immense value in a man. Human souls also differ in rank and worth, and a great soul may overtop a crowd of small ones as a mountain overshadows its foothills.

All the arguments that converge upon the hope of human immortality grow more weighty and impressive as a soul looms upon us in greater magnitude and nobility. We may not have the insight to see that the meanest slave or lowest savage has in him a germ of immortal worth; but when mighty men stride across the stage of the world and achieve works of supreme genius, or put forth deeds that reshape the ages, or win crowns of sublime heroism, or wear the blood-red robes of sacrificial service and suffering and martyrdom, we have a powerful conviction that these souls are of immeasurable worth and were not born to die. Socrates and Plato, Dante and Shakespeare, Cromwell and Lincoln, are too great and precious, we feel, to be extinguished as meteors in the night, and we are satisfied only as we are assured that they are set as stars in the firmament of eternity. These arguments support their claims to endless life, but they also support these arguments.

"I do not know," says Dr. James Martineau in his eloquent *Study of Religion*, "that there is anything in nature (unless it be the reputed blotting out of suns in the stellar heavens) which can be compared in wastefulness with the extinction of great minds; their gathered resources, their matured skill, their luminous insight, earth has been one great altar from which has risen from humanity the worship of God.

The deepest feeling of humanity is its sense of dependence on God, and its greatest need and most urgent cry was voiced by Augustine: "O God, thou hast made us for thyself, and we cannot rest until we rest in thee." In his experience man finds a personal God in prayer and worship, fellowship and obedience. He seeks him by a primal instinct and impulse which drives him to God as hunger and thirst drive him to food and water. He speaks to him with the confidence of a child to a father and pours out his soul to him. He confesses to him his open faults and secret sins and beseeches him for pardon, purity and peace. He looks for indications of God's guidance and follows the gleam. "Thou wilt light my candle." He catches from God visions of right and goodness, ideals of perfection, of duty, of service and sacrifice, of battles to be fought against hosts of darkness, and of a kingdom of truth and right, brotherhood and love, to be built; and he girds himself up for the battle and throws himself into service and pours out of his body and soul the last full measure of devotion. His very sorrows only drive him closer to the throne of grace as he falls on the great world's altar stairs which slope through darkness up to God.

This worldwide, powerful fact of religion is a witness to immortality: for a dominant note in its faith and worship is the hope of eternal life. It is true that faith in immortality is not absolutely essential to some degree of religion. Humanity in its dependence exists and God exists and there would be ground for the relation of worship between them though immortality did not give it the pledge of endless life. Yet religion without this faith would be deprived of its proper completion and crown and especially of the element of eternal value and would thereby fall to an infinitely lower level. The chief strand would be removed from the tie that binds man to God and the power of religion over this life would be immeasurably weakened.

In all worthy forms of religion from the lowest to the highest, this faith has been a clear and steady flame, a fixed polar star. It pervades in some form pagan religions, even pantheistic Hinduism, glimmers in increasing clearness through the Old Testament, and, in the New, life and immortality are brought out of the twilight into the full day and splendor of the teaching of Christ and his apostles. All Christian prayer and praise, faith and fellowship, service and sacrifice are shot through with this hope, and heaven is the completion and crown of the Christian life.

Destroy this faith and Christian worship would wither into silence, and the whole temple of religion would begin to crumble. The Bible would be closed, every missionary would return, the Christian pulpit would have nothing to say on the mystery of life and death, and the grand Christian hymns would be hushed. Whatever truth and worth there is in religion, if it is not all a lie, are pledged to this faith.

2. *The Fatherhood of God.*

The Fatherhood of God is a strong ground for trust in this hope. Pagan faiths as well as the Christian revelation and theistic philosophy teach that human souls are the offspring of God and bear his image and

81

are bound up in fellowship with him. Men are thus the children of God, and he sustains to them the paternal relation, and they to him the filial relation.

This mutual relation involves mutual obligations and fellowship and faithfulness. In begetting human souls God has passed the point of producing physical things, or even partial selves such as the lower animals appear to be, and has brought forth children that are capable of sharing his life and love. Such children, having been begotten, are thenceforth essential elements in the divine life and are, in a degree, necessary to its completeness and satisfaction. "The Father seeketh such to worship him."

God having brought forth his children can never be the same without them. They are not mere means to higher ends, but are ends in themselves with inherent and essential life and worth. They are objects of the Father's eternal love and have their home in his heart. Such a relation is a timeless one and reaches no temporal limit, but runs on, growing richer and sweeter forever. For his own sake the Father will not cast his children to the void.

And the children never can be complete and satisfied without the Father. Without him they are waifs in a fatherless world, infants crying in the night and with no father to hear their cry. God himself has implanted the spirit of childhood in human souls, and will he not be faithful to his own work? To suppose that he is begetting children and endowing them with their capacities and hopes only to disappoint them, as one would blow beautiful iridescent bubbles to see them burst, is to suppose that he is making cruel sport of his children and is a fateful and fearful monster more dreadful than we could believe any human father or demon could be.

"Who can believe," says Martineau in his *Study of Religion,* "that the everlasting Mind fulfills its end by disappointing every other? . . . Is the eternal design of Perfection to be gained by the frustrated aspirations of countless ephemeral generations?" "Will the affectionate God," writes W. R. Alger in his *Doctrine of a Future Life,* "permit the ox-hoof of annihilation to tread in these sparrow-nests of humanity so snugly esconced in the fields of being? Love watches to preserve life. It were Moloch, not the universal Father, that would crush into death these multitudes of loving souls supplicating him for life, dash into silent fragments these miraculous personal harps of a thousand strings, each capable of vibrating celestial melody of praise and bliss." The universal human heart and especially the Christian heart thinks better of God and trusts his promise implanted in its own constitution and certified to by the express teaching and promises of Christ.

> Thou wilt not leave us in the dust;
> Thou madest man, he knows not why,
> He thinks he was not made to die;
> And thou hast made him: thou art just.
> —*Tennyson.*

3. *The Instinct of the Heart.*

Instincts are prophecies. They are hereditary constitutional tendencies and impulses which begin to act automatically when they are aroused by their proper stimulus, and they find in their environment their appropriate means of satisfaction; they express the most primary and fundamental needs of the organism and sustain the life of the individual and of the race. They are prophetic previsions and provisions in the constitution that reach forward into the future and meet with their fulfillment and gratification.

The animal world is full of instincts, and they are often marvels and mysteries that excite our astonishment and defy explanation. The bee builds a honeycomb according to mathematical and architectural principles of a high order. Ants organize and carry on a highly complex social order involving government, officers, workers, agriculturalists, soldiers and slaves, domesticated animals and plants, that rivals man's highest political achievements. Wasps sting spiders and caterpillars in their chief nerve centers so as to paralyze them with a skill involving anatomical and physiological knowledge which Romanes said might be justly deemed the most remarkable instinct in the world.

Birds newly fledged and without previous experience make long migrations and find a more favorable clime. The golden plover, a few ounces of fat and feathers, a tiny engine with a few drops of oil for fuel, breeds in summer in Arctic North America and then drives itself in a marvelous flight of upwards of ten thousand miles and winters in Patagonia. Day and night it wings its way over this vast distance, much of it over the trackless ocean, impelled and guided by the mystery of instinct. Insect and bird and fish and all animals are thus moved by inherited impulses that find their appropriate means of satisfaction, and by this means they live and propagate their kind.

Man is also a creature of instincts, born with his nature packed full of them. Many instincts he has in common with the animals, such as act in the babe and child; others of a higher nature are peculiar to himself. Some begin to act at birth and others develop as they are needed in life; some fulfill their temporary use and then wither away, and others grow with our growth and persist to the end.

Our human instincts have their roots and springs down in our subconsciousness. All our associations, habits, instincts are stored and preserved in this hidden chamber. There is reason to think that this subconscious region is large compared with our conscious life, as seven-eighths of an iceberg is submerged beneath the surface of the sea. Not only our individual experiences, but our whole accumulated heredity is deposited in this deep. We are vastly greater than we know or dream. Our heredity runs back through all the generations to the cave man and on back through geological ages to primal cells. Our souls are stratified structures, full of fossils, like the rocky strata in the crust of the earth. There are deeply buried in us ancient submerged continents and extinct constellations of racial experience, and at times these continents push their peaks up as islands and these constellations fitfully blaze up as faint stars in our consciousness. Abnormal "multiple personalities" are sometimes buried in these mysterious depths. This is the underground world and night life of the soul, full of shadows and ghosts and stars. We were indeed "fearfully and wonderfully made" when "my frame was not hidden from thee, when I was made in secret, and curiously wrought in the lowest parts of the earth" (Ps. 139:14-15).

85

THE CHRISTIAN BELIEF IN IMMORTALITY

The subconsciousness plays a part of immense importance in our life. Up out of this huge cellar come swarming through its trapdoors and back stairways of memory and association the shadows of the past to reinforce the present. Suggestion has the power of tapping this hidden reservoir and letting it gush up in jets of thought and feeling. Everything we put into our life will sooner or later come out of our life. Long years afterward on the most unexpected occasions and in the most startling ways "old, unhappy, far-off things, and battles long ago" will come up out of this dark chamber to strengthen and comfort us, or, like ghosts out of their graves, to trouble and plague us.

Up out of this great racial deep of the soul comes the instinct of immortality. This is an impulse and desire looking towards a future life which is as old and wide as the human race. The evidence for this is written out in many books, a recent weighty one being *Religion and the Future Life,* edited by Professor E. Hershey Sneath, in which eleven authorities, all university professors, adduce the evidence for such universal belief in every age and every part of the world. The editor sums up the evidence in the statement: "One cannot study the history of religions without being profoundly impressed by the fact that belief in the soul's survival after death seems to be almost universal. So eminent an authority as Sir James Frazer says: 'The question whether our conscious personality survives after death has been answered by almost all races of men in the affirmative. On this point skeptical or agnostic peoples are nearly, if not wholly, unknown.'"

This racial human desire and belief has all the marks

of instinct: universality, constitutionality, priority to experience, and necessity in our life. In lowest savagery and highest civilization, grossest superstition and purest religion, in every age and under every sky instinct impels man to cry out of the depths of his heart for immortal life. That it exists or manifests itself in different individuals in greater or less degrees and is almost or altogether wanting in some, is quite in accordance with the moderate variability of instinct and does not invalidate the general fact of its universality.

The human spirit shrinks from extinction and has a mighty passion for life. It stands on the shore of time, peering out over the ocean of eternity that it may discern the green shore of a far new world. This life, rich and glorious as it may be, it holds to be a poor and pitiful fragment without more life. Man buries his dead and refuses to believe that they have vanished into nothingness, but hopes to meet them again. He enters the dark shadow of death triumphantly believing that he will emerge into the eternal morning.

"There are wondrous impulses in us," says W. R. Alger, "constitutional convictions prescient of futurity, like those prevising instincts in birds leading them to take preparatory flights before their migration. Eternity is the stuff of which our love, flying forward, builds its cooing nest in the eaves of the universe. If we saw wings growing out upon a young creature, we should be forced to conclude that he was intended to fly. It is so with man. By exploring thoughts, disciplinary sacrifices, supernal prayers, holy toils of disinterestedness, he fledges his soul's pinions, lays up treasures in heaven, and at last migrates to the attracting clime."

Instincts, we have seen, grow out of and express the most primary and fundamental needs of life; and in nature they find their appropriate means of satisfaction. They are not lies; they are trusted and they tell the truth. The instinct of immortality, we must believe, is of the same nature. It is an expression and outgrowth of the age-long racial need of immortality as the necessary complement and completion of our life, and if it is a true instinct it must be a part which has its counterpart that fits it as the die fits the coin. The belief that it is a true instinct is an act of faith, but it is one to which the race has long committed itself, which is altogether in accordance with the analogy and promise of nature, and to which the very universe has pledged its integrity.

Can it be that the instinct of the ant and bee and bird is true and that of man is false? Will nature lead the world of life up the slope of instinct to higher life and then at its very summit prove traitor to the highest and noblest instinct of all? Will God implant truth in the heart of the very insects and then inveigle his human children into trust in him only to tell them lies? The human race has ever thought better of its God, however dimly and darkly it has seen his face, and it will ever trust the eternity he has set in its heart.

Even those who doubt or deny immortality cannot altogether kill this instinctive hope in their hearts. Thomas H. Huxley, in 1883 when near sixty years of age, wrote: "It is a curious thing that I find my dislike to the thought of extinction increasing as I get older. It flashes across me at all sorts of times with a sort of horror that in 1900 I shall probably know no more than I did in 1800. I had rather be in hell." And arch-agnostic as he was and inventor of the name, yet some belief in a personal God and a wistful if faint hope of immortality appear in the inscription composed by his wife and placed on his tomb by his special direction:

> And if there be no meeting past the grave,
> If all is darkness, silence, yet 'tis rest;
> Be not afraid ye waiting hearts that weep,
> For God so giveth his beloved sleep,
> And if an endless sleep He wills—so best.

The heart speaks by intimation and allusion, suggestion and mystic presentiment, and when its yearning is denied and suppressed, it finds indirect ways of whispering its secret to the soul. Agnostic literature contains many instances in which men that have denied this hope have yet let it unwittingly slip out of them in some byword or chance allusion. When least expected it comes knocking at the door, and before the mind is aware of its presence it has captured the soul This is one of the marks of its truth and power.

> Just when we are safest, there's a sunset touch,
> A fancy from a flower-bell, some one's death,
> A chorus-ending from Euripides,—
> And that's enough for fifty hopes and fears
> As old and new at once as nature's self,
> To rap and knock and enter in the soul.
> —*Browning*.

The poets are the prophets of the heart. They interpret its dreams and see its visions. They can play upon the thousand-stringed harp of the soul and draw from it its deepest chords and mellowest music; and they have ever struck upon its mystic strings the profoundest and noblest notes of immortality. The extinction of the soul does not lend itself to inspiring poetry. Atheism is not singable. But all the great poets have sung the song of immortal hope. There is no snow-capped, sun-bathed mountain peak of poetry that does not reflect this light, caught from a luminary beyond the horizon of this world. An anthology of poetry on death and immortality is a great constellation of stars. And this instinct of the heart is one of the fixed stars of the first magnitude in the firmament of these prophets.

> My own dim life should teach me this,
>   That life shall live forevermore,
>   Else earth is darkness at the core,
> And dust and ashes all that is.
>
> Here sits he shaping wings to fly:
> His heart forebodes a mystery:
> He names the name eternity.
>
> *—Tennyson.*

> Though inland far we be,
> Our souls have sight of that immortal sea,
>   Which brought us hither,
>   Can in a moment travel thither,
> And see the children sport upon the shore,
> And hear the mighty waters rolling evermore.
> *—Wordsworth.*

> I go to prove my soul!
> I see my way as birds their trackless way.
> I shall arrive! What time, what circuit first
> I ask not: but unless God send his hail
> Or blinding fireballs, sleet or stifling snow,
> In some time, his good time, I shall arrive:
> He guides me and the bird. In his good time!
> *—Browning.*

90

RELIGIOUS GROUNDS OF BELIEF

4. *The Incompleteness of the Soul.*

Any unfinished structure suggests and promises that it will be carried to completion. A building half-way up with work actively progressing on it, a portrait only sketched in outline, a poem that is plainly only the first rough draft,—these and all such fragments point with the finger of prophecy and promise to the completed product. God is a builder who does not stop half way in his work, and the prophetic faith of the human heart was expressed by the psalmist in the prayer, "Jehovah will perfect that which concerneth me: Forsake not the work of thine hands."

The human soul is an uncompleted structure, an outline sketch, a growth in its first stages, and its present attainment falls vastly short of its own ideal. What it is is only a hint of what it might be and what it feels it ought to be. The whole soul is a bundle of cravings and faculties, powers and possibilities, physical and mental and spiritual, that are all more or less plastic and germinal. Some of these, such as the procreative passion, do fulfill their purpose, reach their full satisfaction, and are then sloughed off, evolution leaving them behind as withered husks. But others of them reach no such limit and are like parabolic curves which never become closed orbits but ever sweep wider areas, and are thus infinite in their outreach and demands.

Our mental faculties are of this infinite nature. They unfold their tentacles and throw them wider and farther, laying hold of the world with an ever ampler grasp, feeling deeper into its crevices, penetrating to its core and reaching out to the stars, but never approach a limit to their inquiries and processes and powers, or to their capacities of growth, and never attain full and final satisfaction.

Every question the mind solves only discloses a hundred others that are not solved, and thus its conscious ignorance grows faster than its knowledge. The larger is the sphere of its light, the vaster is the surrounding sphere of darkness that shuts it in. Newton himself realized that he had only picked up a few pebbles on the shore of the infinite ocean of truth, and this visible shore has enormously increased its breadth and extended its sweep since his day.

The human mind, immense and splendid as are its present achievements, has only made a beginning. It has innate power to press indefinitely beyond its present boundaries and launch out upon unknown deeps and fathom unsounded depths. It believes there is no fact or far corner, no infinitesimal atom or solar monster, no deepest and darkest mystery in the universe it cannot understand if it can only get its eyes and fingers on it. It feels that a million million years would not exhaust its powers and possibilities and demands eternal school days for its development and satisfaction.

The infinitude of truth is a further assurance that the human intellect will never lose its occupation through finding no more worlds to conquer. It thus has eternity stamped upon its constitution as something that can never complete its education and finish its work and be cast aside as a means that has reached its end. Against the rim of the unknown it ever beats as an imprisoned bird against the bars of its cage. It believes it was made to know and has an instinctive faith that God will yet remove the bars and let it know.

RELIGIOUS GROUNDS OF BELIEF

In a still deeper way the human heart is only a bud and a beginning. Its affectional nature has in it the seeds of immortality as it never outgrows its power of loving and craving for social satisfaction, and clings to its fond object more firmly and tenderly as it approaches the verge of earthly life. The love that binds hearts together in kinship and friendship does not exhaust itself, but grows stronger and sweeter until it is more precious than life itself. It looks beyond the grave and passionately longs for reunion and completion on the other side. To cut this love off and not crown it with endless love would be a fatal imperfection and cruel disappointment in the plan of life.

The moral nature has the same parabolic powers as it starts problems and experiences that never reach their solution and goal in this life, but ever run forward and throw themselves unsolved and unsatisfied into another world. So strong is the demand of conscience, or the "categorical imperative," for a future life as the necessary fulfillment of its needs that Immanuel Kant rested on it as a sufficient foundation for belief in immortality. And the human will does not become a spent force with time, but persists in its plans and ambitions and passions and often puts forth its greatest projects and intensest efforts and energy in the last hours of life.

Goodness is a supreme worth in this world, an essential value that can never fall from its shining eminence as a star in the crown of character. Yet we can in this world attain it only in a partial and imperfect degree. It is a rough stone that we can never cut and polish into a flawless jewel; or rather it is only a germ or bud that can only be partially unfolded and never blooms into the full-blown and glorious flower. Yet it has in it this possibility and power and we feel that it must and will be given time in congenial soil and sunshine to reach its ideal and become the perfect beauty of holiness. Our aspiration toward this ideal is a promise of immortality.

Beauty is another sense of the soul that is here only partially developed and gratified. This is one of our finest faculties and most vivid satisfactions. The highest efforts of human genius and the costliest fabrics of human skill and toil are devoted to the production and enjoyment of beauty. Poetry and painting, sculpture, architecture and music are the most glorious outflowering of the human soul and have enormously enriched our human world and increased the joy of life.

Yet we have only touched the fringe of the many-colored, richly-embroidered, splendid robe of beauty. Nature itself is a boundless display of beauty compared with which the supremest human achievements are poor and pitiful. It is a vast canvas set in a stupendous frame. It encloses the star-sprinkled splendor of the heavens, the frescoed dome of the sky and the gorgeous spectacles of the dawn and the sunset, the sublimity and grandeur of the mountain and the majesty and might and mystery of the sea. There is no depth of ocean or hidden nook in a forest that does not have a profusion of beautiful forms. All nature is drenched and saturated with beauty. It has soaked in among its atoms and stained its ultimate elements; or rather it exudes from its central core and Cause.

All this beauty in nature appeals to the human soul and lures it on with the promise that it will yet rifle the world of this wealth and worth. Man has a great hunger and thirst for beauty and feels that he has a right to full satisfaction at this spring. He has only tasted of this wine of life, only caught gleams and hints of this wonderful world, and he longs for direct sight and splendid vision and glorious satisfaction. And this incomplete development of our sense of beauty is another promise and pledge that it shall not be denied its goal but shall reach full and final fruition.

Truth, Goodness and Beauty are thus three fundamental faculties and essential worths of the human soul that are here only implanted in us as seeds and buds and demand for their full growth an eternal world. These are the balances in which we weigh all our worths and in which the meaning and value of our life consist, not means but ends, the essential virtues and final outcome of life, and if these be lost then all is lost and nothing remains to justify all the toil and travail of this world.

The body reaches the limit of its growth and efficiency and then shrinks to the point of its dissolution, but the soul in its intellect and sensibility and will is bounded by no such limit and has the capacity of endless development and enlargement. It is only in the bud and beginning of its achievements and triumphs even in this life. "All this world," writes H. G. Wells, "is heavy with the promise of greater things, and a day will come, a day of unending succession of days, when beings, beings who are now latent in our thoughts and hidden in our loins, shall stand upon this earth as one stands upon a footstool, and shall laugh and reach out their hands amidst the stars."

The whole soul is thus a prophecy of eternal life, and if this be not fulfilled the world is false in its very constitution and core. "If we are utterly to die with the ceasing of breath," writes W. R. Alger, "then there is an amazing want of symmetry between our endowments and our opportunity; our attainments are most superfluously superior to our destiny. Can it be that an earth house of six feet is to imprison forever the intellect of a Laplace, whose telescopic eye, piercing the unfenced fields of immensity, systematized more worlds than there are grains of dust in this globe?—the heart of a Borromeo, whose seraphic love expanded to the limits of sympathetic being?—the soul of a Wycliffe, whose undaunted will, in faithful consecration to duty, faced the fires of martyrdom and never blenched?—the genius of Shakespeare, whose imagination exhausted worlds and then invented new? There is a vast incongruity between our faculties and the scope given them here. On all it sees below the soul reads 'Inadequate,' and rises dissatisfied from every feast, craving, with divine hunger and thirst, the ambrosia and nectar of a fetterless and immortal world. Were we fated to perish at the goal of three-score, God would have harmonized our powers with our lot. He would never have set such magnificent conceptions over against such poor possibilities, nor have kindled so insatiable an ambition for so trivial a prize of—dust to dust." If these powers and possibilities are not to be fulfilled, then "the soul's proud faculties tell glorious lies as thick as stars."

> Wilt thou not ope thy heart to know
> What rainbows teach, what sunsets show?
> Verdict which accumulates
> From lengthening scroll of human fates,
> Voice of earth to earth returned,

Prayers of saints that inly burned—
Saying, "What is excellent
As God lives is permanent;
Hearts are dust, hearts' love remain;
Hearts' love will meet thee again."

—Emerson.

5. *The Incompleteness of the World.*

The incompleteness of the human soul is matched by the incompleteness of the world, which affords a further confirmation of our faith in immortality. From every point of view this is an unfinished world and bears the marks of being a preparatory institution. It is a workshop in which products are roughly shaped out but not finished, a field in which buds are grown but not fruits ripened, a school in which scholars are taken through the primary grades but not graduated. There is a call for a finishing factory, a harvest field, a higher school and a final home. Man is never complete in this world because this world cannot complete him; and thus this world by its very nature begins a work which only another world can finish.

Especially is this world incomplete and disjointed in its moral and social aspects. Its frightful inequalities and injustices, vice and crime, call for adjustment and judgment. Here the strong oppress the weak, the wicked tempt and contaminate the innocent, "truth forever on the scaffold, wrong forever on the throne," corruption proudly sits in high places and scornfully defies justice, social inequalities unjustly exalt some to ill-gotten wealth and ease and luxury and license, and trample others down into bitter poverty and wrong, crime and vice defy all law and order and decency and soak and saturate the social fabric with incredible corruption and frightful forms of iniquity; and war at times plows up the foundations of society in a world-convulsion, fills the earth and air and sea and depths under the sea with explosives and poisonous gases, "blind furies slinging flames," and thus stabs and gashes the world into one great red wound; and sin has turned the whole of human history into one long tragedy of blood and tears.

Conscience cries out against such a world as a final settlement of human affairs, and, if it can be trusted to tell the truth, there must be another world in which all wrongs are made right. If the whole fabric of our moral life is not an illusion and delusion, but the reality and tragedy we believe it to be, it must issue in a final assize in which retribution and rewards are justly distributed. God is a God of truth and justice and will bring every work into judgment, and judgment has not yet had its day. "There must be another world," says Alger, "where the remunerating processes interiorly begun here shall be openly consummated. Can it be that Christ and Herod, Paul and Nero, Timour and Fénelon, drop through the blind trap of death into precisely the same condition of unwaking sleep? Not if there be a God!" "If death gives a final discharge," says Dr. Martineau, "alike to the sinner and the saint, we are warranted in saying that Conscience has told more lies than it has ever called to their account."

We are not blind to the fact that justice and judgment are in some measure executed in this world and that, as Ruskin says, "every day is a day of judgment and irrevocably writes its verdict in the flames of the west." This world is not all a welter of injustice and unrequited wrong, for, were it so, it could not survive but would destroy itself in dissolution and chaos. Yet it is so far out of joint that if we must face it as a moral finality it turns to irrationality, and it can be understood and justified only as we believe that

> behind the dim unknown,
> Standeth God within the shadow, keeping watch above his own.

Not only does moral evil in this world call for another world of readjustment, but the good in it is also only a beginning and a promise which demand completion. Human civilization shows continued progress, though with periods of stagnation and reaction, from the primitive life of cave men up to the highest summits yet attained. But all that has been done can be better done and is only a promise of what may yet be, and man has ever dreamed of a social order of justice and peace and prosperity and of progress in science and art and character that will immeasurably surpass present realizations.

Yet this prospect must run across the boundary of this world for its final fulfilment. In the very nature of this world imperfection and disappointment will mar its finest and furthest achievements. Only an eternal world built of imperishable elements and pervaded with perfect justice and love can fulfill man's dreams and hopes. The present world "stands as yet half built against the sky" and always will, but in our vision of faith we see it rise into the eternal city of God.

> The facts of life confirm the hope
> That, in a world of larger scope,
> What here is faithfully begun
> Will be completed—not undone.

99

6. *Prophetic Elements in Life.*

Our studies so far have been heading toward the conclusion that there are prophetic elements in life that are not fulfilled in this world. Man is a forward-looking being, his mind and heart are anticipative and expectant. He is not shut up within the present, but has a far horizon and is overarched with a vast dome. He is endowed with the imperial power of creative imagination that is an advance agent of all his achievements and molds the world as plastic stuff. His brain is an architect's office in which are prepared plans and specifications that shape steel and stone and build his physical and moral world, or an artist's studio in which are sketched outlines of immortal character, and visions of eternal destiny are painted.

Man dreams dreams and over his path hover ideals that coax and woo him on to larger and lovelier things. He follows the gleam of these visions, he rises to his ideals, or his ideals lay hold of him and lift him starward from the dust. It is the creative imagination that produces the glories of literature and art and all the great achievements of men. Men of genius are eminently the children of their imagination; they see visions that unveil the beauty of the world, or that transform civilization and build a copy of the city of God on earth, rearing its jeweled walls around our horizon and laying its golden pavements right down under our feet.

Every stage and act of life prepares the way for the next scene. All life is preparatory and prophetic. Youth leads on to maturity, and maturity to later years as the morning leads to noon and noon to evening. Education is preparation. Plowing and planting,

100

business adventure and investment, all plan and purpose draw their meaning and fruitage from the future. Young men laid down their lives in France with a far look in their eyes as a costly and splendid sacrifice which was the necessary price of liberty they could not enjoy. Their blood will be the blessing of a thousand generations yet unborn. Macaulay said that in writing his *History of England* he had his eye on the year 2000 A.D. The human soul in this earthly life is often taking long views that pass beyond the borders of time into the endless future and lay hold on eternity.

This is one of the marks of the greatness of man. The animal has it not. As Burns says, "The present only toucheth it." "Not 'envisaging itself,' not being at once actor, spectator, and critic, 'living in the flashing moment,' not seeing the past and the present and the future separately, this is the highest at which we can put the consciousness of animals, and herein lies the distinction between man and animals which makes the overwhelming difference." "The present alone and isolated," says Sir Oliver Lodge, "would be meaningless to us; we look before and after. Our memories are thronged with the past; our anticipations range over the future; and it is in the past and the future that we really live. We eat, we rest, we work, all with an eye to the future. The present moment is illuminated and made significant, is controlled and dominated, by experience of the past and expectation of the future. Without any idea of the future our existence would be purely mechanical and meaningless: with too little eye to the future—a mere living from hand to mouth—it becomes monotonous and dull."

Where does this principle end? It cannot logically stop at the edge of the grave. Man's plans and activities project themselves across this break and chasm as a bridge springs from its abutment. He is ever laying "great bases for eternity," and his most advanced life-structure at death stands only as a beginning and a promise. The prophetic nature of human life demands a future for its fulfilment.

It may be said, however, that death is too violent a break and deep a chasm to permit the hope of this continuity and completion. But a great and sudden change may seem to be a catastrophic break and yet not interrupt the continuity of law and life. A volcano may silently sleep for centuries and then suddenly explode; yet the explosion was no real rupture of continuity, but was caused by the last pound of pressure that had been long slowly accumulating. The ocean tide may gradually rise against the sand dune along its shore, but at last it reaches a height where it flows over the ridge and invades the continent. A steel railway bridge over a river is of different construction from the earthen bank and stone pier from which it springs, but it carries the same track without a break across the river into a new country.

Death may be the rising tide of life that flows over the bank of the body, or the bridge that crosses the river into another world. It is a critical point in life, but its continuity is unbroken. God has implanted in us this prophetic nature and outlook, and we trust that when it brings us to the limit of this world it will not fail us but will find a passage into a larger world of boundless possibilities.

RELIGIOUS GROUNDS OF BELIEF

Build thee more stately mansions, O my soul,
    As the swift seasons roll!
    Leave thy low-vaulted past!
Let each new temple, nobler than the last,
Shut thee from heaven with a dome more vast,
    Till thou at length art free,
Leaving thine outgrown shell by life's unresting sea.
                —Oliver Wendell Holmes.

CHAPTER VI

THE CHRISTIAN GROUNDS OF BELIEF IN IMMORTALITY

The Christian belief in immortality claims all the grounds for this hope, the natural reasons that make their universal appeal in the world as well as its own more distinctive supports. A building rests on the general strata of rock that run around the earth and yet it also stands on its own special foundation. These two general grounds of belief in immortality, the natural and the Christian, more or less overlap and involve each other, but for our purpose they may be considered separately; and having stated the natural we now proceed to state the distinctively Christian reasons for this faith.

1. *Modern Views of the Bible.*

As the Christian grounds of this belief rest on the Christian Scriptures as their historic basis, it will be in order to take a glance at modern views of the Bible to see if this foundation is still trustworthy. Of course it does not fall within the scope of our study to enter in detail upon the critical reconstruction of the Bible, but only to get a rapid general view of it.

The climatic changes that the scientific spirit has swept over all fields, producing our modern knowledge, has not spared the Bible. It is not a book that could be

104

kept shut up and immune in a sealed cell or glass case as a sacrosanct treasure, but it had to come out into the open and bare its breast to every wind and storm that blows and submit to the same tests as every other book and doctrine. Its sacredness could not shield it from the same searching investigation that has revolutionized science and history and every field of knowledge. It is a book of fact and history and doctrine, and all its contents and claims had to be put through the pitiless processes of criticism that the truth about it might be discovered and established.

And so historical criticism has gone through the books of the Bible endeavoring to discover their origin and authorship and order of production, the circumstances and environment of their time and the purpose of their authors in writing them. Involved in the same process has been the question of the accuracy and trustworthiness of the authors as tested by modern methods. This criticism has resulted in general agreement among scholars as to the main facts, and this critical knowledge has become popularized and widely diffused and has largely shaped the current views of the Bible in all scholarly circles.

Modern criticism has been most radical in its reconstruction of the Old Testament, assigning its books to different times and authors than the traditional ones, but this has had practically no effect upon our Christian belief in immortality as this belief has slight relation to the Old Testament.

As to the New Testament this criticism, while it has been not less thorough, has been far less radical in its reconstruction of it as compared with the Old. It has not shaken but confirmed its books as trustworthy historical documents.

On the historicity of the Gospels it will be sufficient for our purpose to give one of the latest and most authoritative deliverances of critical scholarship. The Rev. Arthur C. Headlam, D.D., now Bishop of Gloucester, but formerly Regius Professor of Divinity in the University of Oxford, in his recent *Life and Teaching of Jesus the Christ,* sums up his long study of the Gospels as follows:

> I have aimed, in the first place, at showing that, accepting the results of modern criticism, there is every reason to think that the subject-matter of the first three Gospels represents the traditions about the life and work of Jesus of Nazareth as they were current in the earliest years of the Christian church. Then, secondly, that it harmonizes with all that we know of the times when Jesus lived and the environment in which he taught. Thirdly, that the teaching of Jesus is harmonious throughout, natural in its language and form to the circumstances and representing a unity of thought transcending anything that had existed before. And then, fourthly, that the life as narrated forms a consistent whole. The result of these investigations is to satisfy myself, at any rate, that we have a trustworthy account of the life and teaching of Jesus.

The Book of Acts is an important document in relation to our subject as it contains the testimony and teaching of Paul, and as to its trustworthiness Professor Kirsopp Lake, an extremely radical critic, says: "On the whole, and considering the character of the book, Acts is a first-rate historical document, and singularly easy to understand, so far as the mere enumeration of events is concerned" (*The Earlier Epistles of St. Paul,* p. 13).

The authenticity of the more important Epistles of Paul is undisputed.

It may be said of the authors of the Bible as a whole and especially of the New Testament that they were competent men with opportunities to know what they relate and with honest intentions to tell us the things they saw or knew or believed to be true. These men stood close to the facts and on summits of vision where they gained knowledge and caught light of the highest spiritual worth to the world, and this fact stands untouched by modern criticism.

This view of the Bible does not depend in any degree on any theory of inerrancy or inspiration, but is drawn directly from the facts. Such theories must be inferred from the facts after they have been critically determined and evaluated, and cannot be injected into or imposed upon them before they have been ascertained and established.

The Bible in our judgment comes out of the modern critical process as good a religious book as ever—and far better. This criticism has brought our conceptions of the book nearer to facts and truth and shown us its development out of human experience as enlightened and guided by the Spirit of God, and thereby has brought the book closer to our own business and bosoms and made it more real and helpful, more human and more divine.

It is with this book as our chief record and witness that we proceed to state the Christian grounds for belief in immortality. These grounds all converge upon and come to one burning focus in Christ. A full statement of this argument can be found written out in many volumes and can here only be condensed into a few points.

2. *The Teaching of Christ.*

"A teacher come from God," was the judgment of a great Jewish doctor of divinity upon Jesus, and the centuries have accepted this verdict and turned the world into his amphitheater in which the nations are listening to his gracious words.

The manner of his teaching was artless, simple, sincere, coming as a living stream out of his own experience, appealing to the experience of his hearers, always bearing the accent of reality and conviction and throbbing with sympathy and earnestness. He taught with authority, not with the arbitrary authority of official station, but with that inherent in self-evident truth. His words were their own witnesses and needed no official claim or station to confirm them.

Universality was stamped upon his teaching. His subjects, however personal and local, were yet universal in their range and application. The smallest matter in his hands became great. He kept clear of provincial and temporary affairs and dealt chiefly with the large and permanent interests of the human soul. The teachings of any ancient author, even the greatest, such as Plato and Cicero, are obsolete on many a page, because they have long since been left behind by the progress of human thought. Science has put them in a pitiable plight. But none of the teachings of Jesus is thus out of date and left behind. His essential words are ever abreast and in advance of the age; and still his sublime saying stands true, "Heaven and earth shall pass away, but my words shall not pass away."

Christ brought life and immortality to light in his teaching. Ancient philosophers indulged in speculations and raised hopes as to life after death, but never reached practical certainty. In a pathetic passage in Plato we are told that in the face of the great darkness and mysteriousness which are round about us in this world, there is nothing for a man to do except to take the best advice he can get as to how to live, and then take his chance—like a man crossing a lonely sea on a raft; "unless," he concludes, "we can find some vessel more safe and solid, some word of God on which we may make this passage more securely." Christ is this very "word of God." He did not speculate and hope but made positive affirmations. He spoke as an eyewitness who had come from the other world and testified to that he had seen. "In my Father's house," he said, "are many mansions; if it were not so, I would have told you; for I go to prepare a place for you. And if I go and prepare a place for you, I will come again and will receive you unto myself; that where I am, there ye may be also." "Jesus, knowing that he came forth from God and goeth to God." The passage between this world and the next was a familiar road to him. He was a traveler returned from the other world which was his eternal home, and he spoke of it with the same certainty as he did of this world. Heaven was literally as real and sure to him as earth.

3. *The Character of Christ.*

We always look back of teaching to the teacher to see how they correspond. Do speech and speaker match and make one music, or does what the speaker is thunder in our ears so loud that we cannot hear what he says? Christ bears this test triumphantly. His character stands behind him as the deep and mellow sound-board that gives volume and sweetness and power to his words.

Sinlessness is broadly stamped upon his character and inwoven into the whole texture of his personality. Christ himself with his pure spirit and sensitive conscience was free from any consciousness of guilt, and he boldly challenged his enemies, "Which of you convinceth me of sin?" and none of them ever met the challenge. Modern critics have fared no better in his presence. On the contrary, some modern skeptical scholars have joined in the eulogy of Christ as a perfect character. David Strauss, who reduced Jesus to the level of his human kind, yet said that he had "a consciousness unclouded by the memory of any sins," and John Stuart Mill declared, "Religion cannot be said to have made a bad choice in pitching on this Man as the ideal representative and guide of humanity." The sinlessness of Christ is a moral miracle that lifts him out of his human kind and crowns him with glory.

Sinlessness is the negative side of his character of which the positive side is holiness. His character is compacted of all virtues raised to their highest power and beauty. Purity, patience and peace, honesty and honor, truth and trust, righteousness and reverence, goodness and gentleness, kindness and courtesy, sympathy, service and sacrifice—all virtues and graces combined in him into a perfect disposition, the one flawless diamond and supremely beautiful character that has ever appeared among men.

A striking and difficult feature of his character is its symmetry. Character is a complex and delicate fabric and is easily thrown out of proportion and balance. It may be strong in one direction and weak in another, highly developed in one faculty or virtue and dwarfed in another, and thus may be ill-proportioned and misshapen.

Christ stands supreme and unique among men as the one perfectly balanced man, having all elements of character blended into harmony and making a full-rounded personality. Complementary virtues that are difficult to combine, such as clear cold reason and warm emotionalism, a rich inner life and an active outer life, and apparently contradictory virtues such as justice and mercy, stern integrity and sweet reasonableness, deep personal convictions and patience and charity towards the convictions of others—these and other complementary graces Jesus combined into balanced harmony and unity.

Another feature of his character is its universality. Every human being is born and grows within the envelope of his age and race and country, and never wholly escapes these limitations. But Jesus is the universal Man. He is the typical and representative Man who is equally at home among all the sons of men. And so age can never wither him nor custom stale his infinite variety. He draws to his side men of every race in affection and trust and devotion. Compared with him the greatest geniuses are local characters and parochial schoolmasters. He looms over all the world as the one universal character and is at home in all ages and lands and among all peoples.

The teacher is always greater than his teaching, and this is preëminently true of the supreme Teacher who is himself his greatest message: his truth is our trust, and

his love is our life. This is why in the Epistles of the
New Testament there is so little use made of the teachings of Christ recorded in the Gospels. No allusion is
made to the Sermon on the Mount or the parables which
we think are so precious and vital. Hardly ever is
Christ quoted, but his person is adored; the reflected
light is disregarded because the gaze is fastened on the
Sun; his sayings are forgotten, but Christ himself is
all in all.

4. *The Divinity of Christ.*

The outstanding fact about Jesus Christ is that he
cannot be construed simply as man or purely as God,
but can be understood only as a unique union of both.
His humanity is seen in his physical body and rational
soul, and in all points he was subject to human conditions. But his divinity equally with his humanity is
displayed and demonstrated in the Scriptures. Not only
his preëxistence, but his eternal existence is affirmed.
Divine names are freely applied to him, and divine attri-
butes and actions are ascribed to him. Words that would
be terribly blasphemous or would indicate insanity if
spoken by a human person, fall from his lips as though
they were perfectly natural to him, and are accepted as
such by his disciples and by succeeding ages. He for-
gives sin and expressly declares that this is an exercise
of divine power. He speaks to man as God, claims
divine worship from men, and declares he will judge the
world. The whole New Testament is saturated with the
divinity of Christ. We can scarcely read a line of it
without encountering some act, statement or allusion
relating to him that is absurd if he be conceived under

purely human terms, and yet his person retains its sanity and consistency and its hold upon the Christian world. All lines of teaching and testimony in the New Testament converge upon the exclamation of the Roman soldier at the crucifixion, "Truly this man was the Son of God."

5. *The Resurrection of Christ.*

We here come to the central ground and foundation stone of the Christian belief in immortality. Our space must here compress volumes into paragraphs, and pages into words.

(1) The resurrection of Christ is the rock on which rests the central column that sustains the structure of historic Christianity. Remove this foundation and the great fabric would fall into ruin. Paul himself staked the whole Gospel upon it: "If Christ be not risen, then is our preaching vain, and your faith is also vain." No resurrection means no divine Christ, but a risen Jesus means a divine Lord and mighty Saviour.

Around and against this rock the waves of criticism have rolled and surged for centuries. No other event in history has been subjected to such thorough and keen investigation. The ablest intellects have supported or attacked it, and the most impartial and pitiless light has been poured upon it. An enormous literature has grown up around it. Yet we believe that to-day it stands unmoved and shows no serious signs of disintegration.

(2) The event was forced into the light at the time it occurred. There are miracles recorded in the Bible that happened in obscure conditions. They derive their support from the general web of divine history into which

they are woven, and little or no specific evidence could be adduced for them singly and separately.

The resurrection of Christ stands on a very different basis. This thing was not done in a corner, but took place in the full light of day under a blaze of publicity and is supported by many witnesses and evidences converging upon it. Explicit facts and arguments are given in proof of it. The New Testament is pervaded with the consciousness of the strategic position and critical importance of this fact and pours around it a flood of light such as illuminates no other event in the Bible.

(3) The Scripture evidence for this fact is abundant, definite, and competent, and has ever been convincing to the great body of Christian scholars and believers. It is narrated in all of the four Gospels, with such differences as might be expected from accounts that are more or less fragmentary and are the impressionistic reports of strange events by highly individualistic reporters. The scholars find difficulty in fitting the narratives together and it may be granted that this cannot be smoothly and satisfactorily done, but this may be due to the fact that parts are missing and much must be allowed to individual points of view. Yet history is always tolerant of such differences without doubting the general fact and truth.

There is no doubt that Jesus Christ was crucified, dead and buried. Three days after his burial some of the devoted women went to his tomb expecting to find his body and were prepared to anoint it, but they were amazed to find the tomb empty, and presently they saw Jesus himself. Other appearances followed during the interval before his ascension, making eleven in all.

114

These witnesses were numerous and competent. The disciples had been with Jesus during his ministry and had become familiar with his form and features and knew him as a friend. They were men of good ability and sound judgment; not learned men, it is true, but practical business men whom it would not have been easy to deceive on a matter of fact.

(4) The most remarkable fact about these witnesses is that they were not expecting a resurrection, at first disbelieved in it themselves, and were convinced of it only after the most searching investigation and tests and indubitable proofs. The theory that the disciples of Jesus under the influence of their passionate devotion to him came to have a purely subjective illusion which led them to believe they had seen him risen, is rendered psychologically impossible by the state of their minds. Such illusions and delusions can grow up only in minds that already have some obsession or prepossession in their favor; they demand congenial soil and propitious circumstances. Nothing of the kind but quite the contrary existed in the case of the disciples. While Jesus had spoken to them of his resurrection, yet they seem not to have understood him, and no such expectation was in their minds. His death was a disaster wholly unexpected by them and was at once followed by the utter collapse of all their hopes. They had trusted that Jesus was he who would redeem Israel and set up his kingdom, but his crucifixion was a death-blow to any such hope and smote them into the dust.

Not only so, but when their Lord was reported risen to them they refused to believe the story and scoffed at it as "an idle tale." These disciples were themselves the first skeptics of the resurrection and were the hardest of men to convince of the fact. Thomas held out for eight days and was persuaded only by a physical demonstration. These facts render a subjective delusion impossible, add immense weight to the testimony of the witnesses and put this event on sure ground.

(5) A witness of special directness and weight is the apostle Paul. He was a man of genius and scholarship who has left his mark on the ages and from every point of view is one of the influential men of the world. At first he was an intensely conscientious and bitter opponent of Jesus and especially of the doctrine of his resurrection and was trying to stamp his name out in blood. He repeatedly tells us the story of his conversion at which the risen Christ appeared to him in a burst of heavenly light. According to some scholars, including Harnack, this was only one year after the death of Christ, and after three years passed in meditation Paul went up to Jerusalem and spent fifteen days with Peter and James, the brother of Jesus (Gal. 1:17-19). What did he go there for? To "visit" Peter, he says, but the word is a strong one and may be translated "to cross-examine" these disciples. "It denotes visits paid to places of interest with a view to getting information about them on the spot" (*Expositor's Greek Testament*). The resurrection must have been the chief point of his inquiry. Thus within four years after the event Paul, having had personal experience in which he believed he saw the risen Christ, spent two weeks in investigating the facts as to the resurrection on the ground in company with eyewitnesses; and he tells us these facts in an epistle the genuineness of which is undisputed. Does

not this take us back close to this event and give us very strong testimony?

Paul in another undoubted epistle gives us a detailed list of witnesses to the fact of the resurrection, adds his own testimony, and solemnly asserts that "if Christ be not risen, then is our preaching vain, and your faith is also vain. Yea, and we are found false witnesses of God; because we have testified of God that he raised up Christ: whom he raised not up, if so be that the dead rise not" (I Cor. 15:1-20).

Here is a man of great ability and logical mind, a trained lawyer, a man of lofty character and distinguished services, who virtually puts himself under oath and with a solemn sense of his responsibility to his own age and to coming generations swears to the reality of this event. How many events, even of historic significance, can produce such testimony?

(6) These witnesses all acted out their belief after this event. Plunged into utter despair by the death of Jesus, they at first gave up all as lost. But suddenly within three days these scattered and fleeing disciples were transformed into masterful men and began to preach with irresistible power that their Lord was risen. Persecution immediately arose, and they bore their testimony at the risk and cost of life itself. Yet they persisted in declaring their knowledge of this fact and not one of them ever retracted it.

Finally, they sealed their testimony with their blood. Only one of them escaped a violent death, and they paid the last full measure of devotion to their risen Lord. Men will die to maintain a fact they know to be true, but they will not die to maintain an alleged fact they know to be false. The tremendous revolution that came over these disciples and clothed them with such mighty power and the solemn seal they set to their testimony are explicable only on the theory that they told the truth.

(7) Historical events gather credibility from their environment. They must fit into the facts of their time and be of a piece with the general web of events to which they belong. If they are unrelated to such events and refuse to match them they are thereby discredited, or rendered difficult of proof; but if they bear the same relation to their environment as a key to a lock, their proof becomes relatively easy. The resurrection of Christ is a key to the great lock of history and of divine purpose in the world. The ages prepared the way and grew into readiness for it. It was the outcome and climax of a great plan that was foreshadowed in prophecy and developed in history. Granted that God so loved the world that he gave his only begotten Son to redeem it, his resurrection from the dead as a link in the chain of this redemption becomes normal and natural. The resurrection is the logical completion and glorious crown of the cross, without which the cross would have been final defeat. Torn out of its place it would be hard to prove, but in its place it is logically deserving of belief. If this event were offered to us as a mere wonder, we might reject it; but as a part of a worthy and wondrous plan we are constrained to accept it. It would be hard for us to believe this of any other human being, but it is easy to believe it of Christ. The evidences prove his resurrection, but he also proves the evidences. It is the dynamic Person of Christ that puts sufficient

power behind this event to make it acceptable to our faith. The resurrection was the natural and normal thing for him to do.

(8) History matches this event. The New Testament literature issued out of it as a stream from its fountain. These books were written, not primarily for controversial purposes to prove a theory, but as the expression of a belief and a life. This literature did not create belief in the resurrection, but belief in the resurrection created this literature. The books written about Niagara did not create Niagara. The books of the New Testament are simply straws in the wind which show which way it is blowing, or they are bits of literature floating on a deep and powerful current of history that came gushing out of this event.

Not only did these books issue out of this fountain, but so also did the whole Christian movement and all these nineteen centuries of Christian history. The Gospel ran around the Mediterranean shore, pervaded the Roman Empire, helped to undermine and supersede the whole outworn fabric of the ancient world, and breathed into humanity a new spirit that has shaped our modern ideals and institutions. The doctrine that was the dynamic of this tremendous epochal movement and revolution was the resurrection of Jesus Christ from the dead.

Christendom is a mighty monument that requires an adequate origin and cause, as certainly as the Mound at Waterloo, or the Arch of Titus in Rome. Something happened back there on that first Easter morning that is great and powerful enough and divine enough to account for all these consequences, and this event and this cause we believe was nothing less or else than the resurrection of Jesus Christ.

(9) We can make only a brief reference to inadequate explanations of the resurrection. These erroneous theories began on the very morning of the event (Matt. 28: 11-15), and some of them are now quite obsolete and have been consigned to the grave without hope of resurrection. Buried in this grave are the theory of conscious fraud and the theory that Jesus was not dead on the cross and later revived.

The most generally accepted and plausible theory adopted by those who reject the reality of the resurrection is some form of subjective illusion or delusion. Pure delusion, we believe, is rendered psychologically impossible by the mental state of the disciples.

Sometimes the "vision theory" is stated in terms that may approach or even contain the truth. Thus Schmiedel, one of the ablest supporters of a vision theory, says: "Appearances of the risen Jesus did actually occur; that is to say, the followers of Jesus really had the impression of having seen him." This raises the question as to the nature of the body which Jesus had after his resurrection. Plainly it was not his former body of flesh and blood, for it had spectral and illusive qualities, passing through solid walls and appearing and disappearing in a way impossible to an ordinary human body. The appearance that Christ presented to Paul, also, was not an earthly body, and Paul's description of the resurrection body as "spiritual" denotes something other than a body of flesh and blood, which he declared could not enter the kingdom of God.

The body of the risen Jesus may have been in a transition state adapted to his temporary sojourn with his disciples during the brief period intervening between the resurrection and the ascension. The facts do not call for or permit an unmodified physical body, and the risen Jesus may have appeared to his disciples in a way that presented to them a vision of an apparition, and some statements of the vision theory approach this view. The problem of the nature of this body must ever remain unsolved, and while it leaves room for a vision in the form of an apparition, yet this apparition must be an objective reality and not merely a subjective illusion.

There are those who think they can keep the value of the resurrection of Jesus while they surrender its objective reality. But this seems like trying to keep the tree with its fruit after severing it from its root, or to keep the light after putting out the lamp. If the disciples in their belief in the resurrection were simply hugging a pure delusion, then we cannot permanently profit by their baseless belief, for this would be clinging to the shadow of an exposed illusion, a delusion raised to the second degree of credulity. If they were deluded about the resurrection and it had no objective reality, it can have no logical value for us.

Yet it must be admitted that some Christian believers, under the pressure of modern thought, do abandon belief in a literal resurrection and yet hold that something as yet unexplainable happened on that Easter morning that assured the disciples and may assure us of the persistence if not the personal presence of the ever-living Christ who could not be holden of death. We would not deprive any one of any help to faith in Christian immortality or of any comfort that may be derived from this view. In this mystery we need to leave large room for mutual liberty and charity; and preëminently in this matter, in the spirit of Paul, "Let each man be fully assured in his own mind."

Most if not all the theories that deny the objective resurrection of Jesus have their real root in the denial of the supernatural. They view the resurrection as a violation of a closed and rigid system of physical laws which cannot be invaded and ruptured by such an event. But this concept of nature is becoming belated in philosophy if not also in science. Science more and more along with philosophy is uncovering the spiritual basis of the universe and dissolving it into a system of thought. If we view nature, not as an inflexible mechanism, but as a living organism in which God is immanent, then physical laws are the habits of the divine will and subject to larger divine purposes. According to this view, the resurrection of Christ violated no law but fulfilled a high purpose and was a supremely rational event. It moved in a higher region of reason than we know.

(10) There always have been and doubtless will be dissentient views and voices on the question of the reality of the resurrection of Christ. Such differences are not always explainable on rational grounds and may be rooted down in the secret of personality. A fundamental fact in this connection is that every sincere thinker has a right to his own faith, and then he should leave around it a broad margin of toleration and respect and charity for other views. Every believer in the rationality of the universe and goodness of God must believe that in spite of difficulties and uncertainties the ultimate truth on this subject is greater and more

glorious than we can know or dream. The day will reveal it.

It would avail little to quote names on either side, but we conclude this part of our discussion with two weighty quotations, one from an eminent scientist and the other from an able theologian.

The first is from the recent work of James Y. Simpson, Professor of Natural Science in New College, Edinburgh, entitled *Man and the Attainment of Immortality*. After tracing the evolutionary origin of man and considering the Scriptural doctrine of immortality, he comes to the resurrection of Christ and says:

Now the proof of all this is our Lord and Saviour Jesus Christ. It was natural for the apostles to correlate immortality with him because he was perfectly good, and, as a matter of simple fact, he brought life and immortality to light. As related to the disciples, the Resurrection implies their objective certainty that he whom they had known and loved, and with whom they had companied in the days of his flesh, was still alive and communicating to them the mind of God, and his purpose for the world. The basis of the Resurrection faith was not so much the Empty Tomb as the conviction of the disciples that in these post-resurrection experiences they had been seeing, hearing, and speaking with the same historic Personality whom they had followed during these three years, and thought they had lost forever. At the same time, the fact that we are just beginning to understand the effects of mind and particularly of emotion upon the metabolism and actual constitution of the body, that we are only on the threshold of our knowledge of what is involved in the far from static conception of personality, and that we have no ability whatever to estimate what would be the effect of a sinless spiritual life upon its physical concomitant, forbids us to relegate the story of the Empty Tomb to the realm of legend. However regarded, the Resurrection is the supreme proof of the triumph of spirit over matter.

The second quotation is from a recent critical work, Dr. W. W. Wade's *New Testament History*. This thorough scholar and impartial critic after examining all the literature and facts in the case holds to the objective reality of the resurrection and comes to this conclusion:

Thus the available evidence, in the case alike of the Eleven Apostles and of St. Paul, points to the conclusion that the accounts of their visions of the Risen Christ are not mere dramatic expressions of intellectual convictions attained solely by reasoning and reflection, but that certain visions were creative causes of those convictions.

6. *Christ and Immortality.*

It remains to sum up and apply the facts as to Christ in their relation to immortality.

The principle of the special worth of great souls, already set forth, comes to its highest expression and power in Christ. He taught as never man taught, exhibited a sinless and altogether perfect character, and stepped unharmed through the doorway of death and came back to bear witness to the other country. He wrought a work and achieved a character that are supreme and unapproachable among men.

As he now stands before us, set in the vast framework of the centuries, he is a lofty and sublime Figure and shines the Master of the world. He has breathed his spirit through the ages and is reshaping their institutions; he laid a spell upon the centuries and they have acknowledged his sway and swung their orbits around him as their gravitative center and organizing power. Christendom to-day, however partially and imperfectly as yet, is stamped with his image and superscription. It dates its calendar from his birth and weighs its institutions, laws, literature and life in his balances. His sayings are the seeds of our modern world, and more and more will they spread and bloom on every shore.

All our arguments for immortality converge upon him as in a focus and there burn in their greatest intensity and power. These arguments prove his immortality, but much more does he prove these arguments. If that Great Soul and White Spirit vanished in the night of death and left only a handful of dust under the Syrian stars, then we feel that we live in an irrational world which devours its noblest children and betrays all its promises. The human mind will ever refuse to believe in such a wreck of reason and of hope.

In the resurrection of Christ we have a demonstration of the other world and the immortal life. His empty tomb is an open door through which pours a flood of light into this world. To those who believe in this fact and stand in its illumination immortality has passed from the region of speculation and hope into light and knowledge. In Christ all the scattered dim rays of instinct and reason and faith converge to their focus in Him who brought life and immortality to light.

> I gather up the scattered rays,
> Of wisdom in the early days,—
> Faint gleams and broken, like the light
> Of meteors in a Northern night,
> Betraying to the darkening earth
> The unseen sun which gave them birth;
> I listen to the sibyl's chant,
> The voice of priest and hierophant;
> I know what Indian Kreshna saith,
> And what of life and what of death

THE CHRISTIAN BELIEF IN IMMORTALITY

The demon taught to Socrates,
And what, beneath his garden trees
Slow-pacing, with a dream-like tread,
The solemn-thoughted Plato said;
Nor lack I tokens, great or small,
Of God's clear light in each and all,
While holding with more dear regard
Than scroll of heathen seer or bard
The starry pages, promise-lit,
With Christ's evangel overwrit,
Thy miracle of life and death,
O Holy One of Nazareth.

—*Whittier.*

CHAPTER VII

ETERNAL LIFE

We have been moving in our arguments along two main roads leading to belief in immortality: the natural and the revealed grounds of this hope, or nature and revelation, science and Scripture; and these two now converge and meet in a view of the nature and conditions of eternal life that is a solid and satisfying conclusion of all our reasonings.

1. *The Voice of Science.*

Herbert Spencer, in his *Principles of Biology,* Chapters IV-VI, has worked out with remarkable insight and luminous exposition the scientific grounds and nature of eternal life and has not hesitated to draw the conclusion. "Perfect correspondence," he declares, "would be perfect life. Were there no changes in the environment but such as the organism had adapted changes to meet; and were it never to fail in the efficiency with which it met them; there would be eternal existence and universal knowledge." "Eternal existence and universal knowledge,"—what is this but eternal life? Here, it would appear, on the ground of nature itself we are reaching our goal. This eminent naturalistic philosopher has taken his place among the prophets, and science is at last speaking the very language of faith.

127

THE CHRISTIAN BELIEF IN IMMORTALITY

That life depends on correspondence with environment is an obvious fact, open to the layman as well as to the biologist, although science enormously enlarges and illuminates our knowledge of this relation. Any living organism from the lowest single-celled plant or animal up to man can exist only as it is able to adapt itself to its environment of soil and air and temperature, food and light, activity and rest, and subtle chemical and physiological conditions. The microbe has a very narrow environment and only a slight power of adjusting itself to changes in it. It touches the world at only a few points, and a small change in temperature or food supply extinguishes its life. As life rises in the scale from single cells to higher forms the organism increases in complexity and is dependent on a correspondingly more complex environment with an increased power of adjustment to it. The fish has for its environment the river or ocean, and the fox has the forest. The immensely higher organization of these vertebrates brings them into dependence upon an enormously more complex environment, and they also have greater plasticity for adjusting themselves to environmental changes. We also see a progression in the course of evolution from a lower to a higher environment. The first life was apparently born in the sea, and there it developed its organisms until they began to emerge from the water out upon the land and up into the air. The lung-breathing animals are of a higher type than the gill-breathing and live in a wider and freer environment.

This principle reaches its highest expression in man whose organism stands at the top of the scale and whose environment has become the earth and solar system and

128

stars. He also has the largest capacity, on the whole, of adapting himself to changes. He can live in tropic heat or in arctic cold, on the land or on the water and even under the water and up in the air, on the plain or on the mountain, and can utilize an immense variety of food materials. His mental powers also enable him to contrive all manner of artificial adjustments and substitutes and cunning inventions and desperate devices by which he can adapt himself to changes in his environment, and thus he combats heat and cold, famine, fire and flood, disease and death. Man in a measure is master of his environment and thus he protects and prolongs his life.

But death finally comes to man. Just what is its natural cause the biologists have not yet clearly determined. Though man may keep himself in the most favorable physical conditions, yet in time his organism undergoes changes he cannot avoid or resist and death is the inevitable result. These changes, however, are due to some lack of plasticity or power of the organism to maintain its adjustment to its environment. Could this correspondence be perfectly maintained in a perfect environment death would never result, and man would attain to "eternal existence and universal knowledge," or earthly immortality.

The earthly environment, however, is not perfect. It is never in a state of fixed equilibrium, but is ceaselessly swept with storms and waves, changes of temperature and humidity, fluctuations in nourishment, and with disease, that constantly strain and rack the human body and tend to wear it out and overcome its power of adjustment and that finally compass its dissolution. And these continual, comparatively minute changes will

129

eventually accumulate and culminate in such great changes of climatic and continental conditions as will greatly modify human life, or render its continuance on this planet impossible. And finally these secular changes will destroy the planet itself and dissolve the very solar system.

Full and final eternal life in this world, constituted as it is, is therefore unattainable. Life here does not find a perfect and permanent environment, and it does not have a perfect and perpetual power of adjustment. But give it this perfect environment and endow it with perfect plasticity, and then biology itself asserts it will have "eternal existence and universal knowledge," or eternal life.

2. *The Voice of Revelation.*

Having heard the voice of science on the nature of eternal life, we now turn to the voice of revelation in Scripture. What did Jesus, the Lord of Life, say that eternal life is? "And this is life eternal, that they might know thee the only true God, and Jesus Christ, whom thou hast sent" (John 17: 3). Here we have another definition of eternal life, which is yet not another but is fundamentally the same with that of science. Eternal life consists in knowledge, and knowledge is correspondence with environment. Our human life, physical, mental, social, moral and religious, has its root and continuance in correspondence.

Knowledge is the mental correspondence of our thoughts with things, of our ideas with reality. We know reality in all its forms and activities and laws as we get our conceptions into correspondence and harmony

130

with these things so that our ideas fit into and interwork with them as cogs in one wheel fit into and work together with the corresponding cogs in another wheel. Thus we get into correspondence with the earth down to its atoms and electrons, and with the whole heavens out through the solar system to the stars and nebulæ. The wider and deeper is our knowledge of these things the broader and closer is our correspondence with them and power over them and the greater and richer is our life.

In a similar way, our life consists in our knowledge of and harmony with our social and esthetic, moral and religious environment. The more widely and deeply we know and enter into relations with our fellow human beings the broader and richer is our social life. And how enormously does our knowledge of beauty in nature and art, mountain and sea, music and painting and sculpture, enlarge and enrich our life? To know these things is to get into correspondence with them and enjoy them as they grow incorporate with our very souls. Our moral knowledge broadens and deepens our life with still higher relations and enriches it with still more precious worths. And this process reaches its highest application and logical limit in our religious knowledge which brings our life into correspondence with God's life and fills us with the infinite fullness of his truth and beauty and blessedness. It is thus that, as Wordsworth tells us,

> With an eye made quiet by the power
> Of harmony, and the deep power of joy,
> We see into the life of things.

And this leads us right up to Christ's own definition of eternal life and shows us that his idea of it was no arbitrary view of his own, out of relation to reality and foreign to all our modern science and psychology, but was right in line with these and is still ahead of them. This is true of all his teachings; they are not peculiar religious doctrines, ancient dogmas long since obsolete, or subjective conceptions remote from all our modern thinking, but they are rooted down in nature and are the eternal laws of life. We are only beginning to catch up with them.

This is life eternal to know God, and Jesus Christ, whom he hath sent. Eternal life is correspondence with God. Paul expresses the same thought when he says that our life is hid with Christ in God; and this conception of eternal life runs all through the Bible and comes out in many forms of expression.

All our life is correspondence with God, who is our true and all-comprehensive environment. Our physical life must correspond with his physical laws, or it cannot endure an instant. Our mental life corresponds with his mind so far as our ideas are true; and these true ideas let us into God's life and out into his liberty. The meaning of all the marvelous modern sciences and magic machines, astronomy and geology and physics, railway and steamship, telegraph and telephone and radio, automobile and airship, is just this, that we are getting to know God more fully, growing into broader and finer correspondence with him, and are so far sharing his knowledge and power and freedom, his splendid life and glorious liberty.

So, also, our esthetic knowledge lets us into the beauty of God. That God is beautiful is a frequent thought of Scripture, and all the beauty of the world exudes from his nature. The mountain is but a suggestion of his majesty, the sunset but a gleam of his glory, and the constellations are but the golden fringes of his garment. All musical chords and melodies, themes and compositions, are but echoes of the eternal song in his heart. The artist knows God intimately at this point, and art is one of the richest paths into his life. So also does our social and moral experience let us into the life of God. God is love, which is the bond and soul of social life, and he is righteousness, which is the ground of moral life, and in so far as we know these relations we correspond with him.

This brings us to the supreme expression of this principle. Our religious or spiritual life is our conscious knowledge of and correspondence with God. Our relation to God on the lower levels of knowledge may be unconscious, but when it enters the region of conscious faith and fellowship it becomes religion in the proper sense. This higher knowledge is not contradictory to or incongruous with the lower unconscious relation, but is its full flowering out and finest blossom and ripest fruit. It brings our life into its widest and deepest and fullest correspondence with God. It removes the obstruction and hindrance, the rebellion and blindness of sin and harmonizes the soul with the holiness and will of God. It tunes the soul into unison with God at every point, physical, mental, social, esthetic, moral and spiritual, so that all its strings vibrate in harmony with him, and his life slips through it as music through a flute or as strains flow from an organ. All life swells into its fullest and finest, richest and sweetest as we know God and Jesus Christ, whom he hath sent.

133

Christ is the incarnation of God, God come down to us so that we can see him and enter into fuller relations with him. As we know Christ we know God, and as we live in the spirit of Christ we live the life of God. This process is going on through all the activities and means of the Christian life, and it reaches its completion when our lives are hid with Christ in God, perfectly harmonized with him, so that we live and yet not we but Christ liveth in us and we are filled with all the fullness of God.

Our life lies embedded in nature and ensphered in an infinitely wider and vaster world. The real environment of our life is God. All material forms of our environment, rocks and roots, soil and showers and sunshine, earth and sun and stars, are but elements or aspects of this wider and final environment. God is not far from us or external to us, but nigh us, even in our hearts. "In him we live and move and have our being." "Closer is he than breathing, nearer than hands and feet." The immanence of God has been emphasized in our modern thinking in both science and philosophy as well as in theology.

We then have in God and Christ a perfect environment, meeting and matching our life at every point, and subject to no changes, but the same yesterday, to-day and for ever. Our spiritual life is also capable of maintaining perfect correspondence with this perfect environment. Sinless purity and filial faith and fellowship will never permit the soul to fall out of harmony with God but will ever fold it closer to his heart and hide it deeper in his life.

Mr. Spencer's own definition of "eternal existence and

universal knowledge" is thus fulfilled in the Christian life. Nature and revelation, science and Scripture, here unite and speak with one voice as to the nature of that life which contains no seed of death and will endure forever.

3. *Eternal Life a Timeless Relation.*

It is to be observed that the deepest mark of eternal life is not simply endless existence: it is perfect correspondence; it is not a matter of quantity but of quality; not a relation to time, but a relation to God. It transcends time and may be merged in some higher eternal state. We have some hint of this even now in our consciousness which overleaps the present into the past and future and refuses to find any limit to its forward look.

Living is never mere lasting. A giant Redwood may be three thousand years old, but it does not have as much life in thirty centuries as a babe has in a month or a minute. Life is not measured by the circle of the sun or by the longer circles of the stars. "We live in deeds, not years; in thoughts, not breaths; in feelings, not in figures on the dial." Better fifty years of Europe than a cycle of Cathay, and one crowded hour of glorious life is worth an age without a name. Eternal life is harmony with God, and this crowds the soul, not simply with years, though all the process of the sun and cycles of the stars are included in it, but with spiritual wealth and worth, with the noblest thought and feeling, sympathy and service and song.

Eternal life therefore is a present possibility and possession. It is not simply an attainment that may be realized only when we have passed beyond time into eternity. It is not a relation to time at all, but to God, and we may enter into it now. "This *is* life eternal, that they might know thee the only true God, and Jesus Christ, whom thou hast sent." "And this is the record, that God hath given to us eternal life, and this life is in his Son. He that hath the Son, hath life."

Nevertheless, the perfect correspondence with God which is eternal life will not be fully and finally realized in this world. It cannot be so realized here because the roots and remnants of sin still remain in us and also because we are now in part related to and correspond with the earthly, fleshly and fleeting environment. This environment, which includes the body, can never be the basis of eternal life because it is not itself eternal. It is ever passing away from us, and we must presently pass away from it. But death marks the severance of the soul from this temporal environment and ushers us directly into the perfect environment of God, the final basis of eternal life.

How much of our present life will go with our body, whether its senses and sensational experience will be shed along with the flesh, and the spirit be liberated into some higher type of knowledge and life, we cannot now know. But there are intimations of such higher knowledge in both nature and revelation. Evolution has been constantly lifting life from lower to higher types, from the microbe to the vertebrate, from the gill-breathing water animal to the lung-breathing air animal, and so on up to man. This line of ascent points on up to still higher forms, and the human soul may be only the germ and prophecy of life as much above this present form as the swift-winged, gorgeously-arrayed butterfly is above the slow-crawling, shaggy caterpillar.

Scripture points in the same direction. It is full of intimations and pictures and promises of a higher life than we can now know or conceive. "Beloved, now are we the sons of God; and it doth not yet appear what we shall be: but we know that, when he shall appear, we shall be like him; for we shall see him as he is" (I John 3:2). "Now this I say, brethren," writes Paul, "that flesh and blood cannot inherit the kingdom of God; neither doth corruption inherit incorruption" (I Cor. 15:50). And equally significant is the declaration of Jesus that "in the resurrection they neither marry, nor are given in marriage, but are as the angels of God in heaven" (Matt. 22:30).

These Scriptural statements all point to a life released from sense and liberated into pure spirit. No doubt the spirit will have a spiritual body or an organism or means of relation to its environment, but it will not be like this "muddy vesture of decay" that has been so infected and loaded with the seeds of evil and death and has been the means of so much sin and sorrow in the earthly life. We are here on the borders of a mystery we cannot penetrate for we cannot conceive of that which lies beyond our experience.

Such correspondence with God and Christ will be pure life and liberty, beauty and blessedness. Then will our "mouth be filled with laughter and our tongue with singing." "Lift up your eyes to the heavens, and look upon the earth beneath; for the heavens shall vanish away like smoke, and the earth wax old like a garment, and they that dwell therein shall die in like manner:

but my salvation shall be for ever, and my righteousness shall not be abolished." Then shall eternal life begun here be completed there, and "neither death, nor life, nor angels, nor principalities, nor powers, nor things present, nor things to come, nor height, nor depth, nor any other creature, shall be able to separate us from the love of God, which is in Christ Jesus our Lord." "There is no death: what seems so is transition."

> There is no death! The stars go down
>   To rise upon some fairer shore,
> And bright in heaven's jeweled crown
>   They shine forevermore.
>
> And ever near us, though unseen,
>   The dear immortal spirits tread;
> For all the boundless Universe
>   Is life—there is no dead.
>
> —*J. L. McCreery.*

The rise of man is endless. Be in hope:
  All stars are gathered in his horoscope!
The brute man of the planet, he will pass,
  Blown out like forms of vapor on a glass,
Child of the higher skies will rend his bars,
  Laugh and reach out his hand among the stars.

CHAPTER VIII

PRAGMATIC TESTS AND CONFIRMATIONS

How does belief in immortality stand the various tests that may be applied to it? What is its effect and value in practical life? Does it make any difference whether it is true or not? And is any difference it makes good or bad? To these pragmatic tests must this question come.

1. *Does It Win the Assent of Scientific Men?*

How stands this question among scientific men? While this is a question that each one must decide for himself, being "fully assured in his own mind," yet we are rightly influenced in no small degree by men of special knowledge and logical power who speak with some degree of authority. Scientific men are truth-seekers of special ability and training and impartiality, and their views on any subject falling within their domain are entitled to great weight. If they cast their votes solidly against the belief in immortality, the fact would be a very serious one for the believer in this hope. The truth is, however, that they are not at all unanimous on one side or the other, but are divided very much as other people are. This indicates that the question is not one that can be demonstrated or decided by strictly scientific methods but is one of those larger questions that involve faith and the mystic moods of the heart and yearnings of the soul.

Efforts have been made to subject the question to statistics and tabulation. A few years ago the American branch of the Society for Psychical Research conducted a questionnaire on the future life, and out of 329 replies received, only 33 per cent felt "the question to be of urgent importance to their mental comfort," and only 22 per cent "desired a future life whatever the conditions might be."

On the other hand, the London *Daily Telegraph*, in 1904, conducted in its columns a long correspondence on the subject, and the editor summed it up in the conclusion: "I should imagine that so far as this correspondence reflects the mind of the English people, the believers must be ten or twelve times as numerous as doubters, and this, too, in an age which has evidently been rashly styled a skeptical one."

These questionnaires, however, were addressed to general classes and not specially to scientific men. Dr. James H. Leuba, of Bryn Mawr College, in 1916 conducted such a questionnaire with about five hundred scientists and students, and the replies indicated that "the number of believers in God, in every class of persons investigated, is less, and in most instances very much less, than the number of non-believers," and "the number of believers in immortality is somewhat larger than in a personal God." A more detailed examination of Dr. Leuba's answers shows that about one-third of his scientists believe in immortality, one-third doubt it, and one-third disbelieve it. This indicates that two-thirds of his correspondents at least admit the possibility of immortality.

These results are disappointing and disquieting enough, but there is less value than at first appears in such statistical investigations, as Dr. Leuba's questions and replies both show that there is necessarily such vagueness in the meaning of such questions that careful thinkers are cautious about responding to them with a brief dogmatic answer that is so easily misunderstood. Dr. Leuba's interpretation of some of the answers he received has also been questioned.

This faith has always been attended with doubt, as light is with shadows, and no doubt agnosticism and evolution in their first effects before their bearing was better understood did spread a mist over this hope so that "there has been for years a steady ebb from the shores of another life." Both science and philosophy, however, have thrown such light on agnosticism that it has lost its terror and been in no small degree discredited, and on evolution so as to turn it from being a foe to a friend of this hope.

A faith that commands the assent and avowal of such distinguished scientists as Newton and Laplace and, among moderns, of Asa Gray and James D. Dana, Charles A. Young and Alfred Russel Wallace, Lord Kelvin and Sir Oliver Lodge, J. Arthur Thompson and James Y. Simpson and Robert A. Millikan; among philosophers, of Plato and of a long roll of the most eminent modern philosophers, Descartes and Leibnitz, Immanuel Kant, Lotze, and many of our own day; and among psychologists, who are supposed to have most difficulty on this subject, of such preëminent men as James and Münsterberg and Ward, cannot encounter contradictions and hostility in science, but must rather meet with a friendly attitude and encouragement.

In connection with the meeting of the American Association for the Advancement of Science in 1922 the Executive Committee, representing its 12,000 members, issued a statement in which they affirmed the fundamental harmony of science and religion. In 1923 a similar statement was issued by thirty-five eminent thinkers in religion and science in which they affirm: "Each of these two activities represents a deep and vital function in the soul of man, and both are necessary for the life, the progress, and the happiness of the human race. It is a sublime conception of God which is furnished by science, and one wholly consonant with the highest ideals of religion, when it represents Him as revealing Himself through countless ages in the development of the earth as an abode for man and in the age-long inbreathing of life into its constituent matter, culminating in man with his spiritual nature and all his God-like powers." Among the names of fifteen distinguished scientists signed to this statement are those of Henry Fairfield Osborn, Paleontologist, President of the American Museum of Natural History, New York; Edwin Grant Conklin, Zoologist, Head of the Department of Zoology, Princeton University; James Rowland Angell, Psychologist, President of Yale University; George David Birkhoff, Mathematician, Head of the Department of Mathematics, Harvard University; William Henry Welch, Pathologist, Director of the School of Hygiene, Johns Hopkins University; John Merle Coulter, Botanist, Head of the Department of Botany, University of Chicago; Michael I. Pupin, Physicist, Head of the Department of Electromechanics, Columbia University; William Wallace Campbell, Astronomer, Director of Lick Observatory and President of the University of California; and Robert A. Millikan, Physicist, Director of Norman Bridge Laboratory of Physics, Pasadena.

More recently still (September, 1924) at the opening of the American Chemical Society, at Cornell University, Sir Max Muspratt, an eminent English chemist, delivered an address on "Chemistry and Civilization" in which he uttered a note of warning against materialism so solemn that it sounded as though it were being delivered from a pulpit, as indeed it was, a pulpit that was heard throughout the country and the world. "The greatest danger that is threatening civilization today," he said, "is materialism. The growth of materialism has far outdistanced the mental and spiritual development of man." "Spiritual" is a rather unusual word to fall from the lips of a scientist in a scientific address, but it is the very word he used.

There is much and growing evidence that in recent years in the higher circles of thought the tide has turned from agnosticism and materialism toward Christian faith and the immortal hope.

> And verily many thinkers of this age,
> Aye, many Christian teachers, half in heaven,
> Are wrong in just my sense, who understood
> Our natural world too insularly, as if
> No spiritual counterpart completed it,
> Consummating its meaning, rounding all
> To justice and perfection, line by line,
> Form by form, nothing single or alone,
> The great below clenched by the great above.
> —*Mrs. Browning.*

2. *Is It Confirmed by Spirit Communications?*

Can belief in immortality produce the pragmatic proof of spirit communications? Have any voices reached us from the other world? The belief in such communications from departed spirits is very ancient and primitive and once filled the world. But such belief has long since shrunk in civilized lands, and in educated circles has been superseded by general doubt and common denial. Shakespeare has made us familiar with "the undiscover'd country from whose bourn no traveler returns," and Robert Ingersoll, standing by the coffin of his dead brother, gave eloquent and pathetic expression to the same view. "Life," he said, "is a journey between the cold silent peaks of two eternities over which no message has ever floated from the other side. Stand we ever so close to the edge of the grave, listen we ever so intently, we cannot hear the whisper of a voice or the rustle of a wing."

A question, however, of such ancient lineage and persistent appeal and compelling interest cannot be suppressed or quieted, but will ever raise its head and make itself heard. Great prejudice has become associated with it because of the mass of superstition and mercenary deception and fraud that have attended it. The whole subject of spirit communications is notorious for its impostures which have deluded countless dupes and victims.

Nevertheless, the question whether some reality lies behind all these reported phenomena remains and should be investigated. Men of science and educated people generally were slow to look into the matter because of its disreputable associations, but this attitude cannot always

144

continue and is now changing. The truth-seeker must ever say, "I am a man, and nothing pertaining to man is foreign to me."

Within recent times the subject has been brought within the field of scientific investigation. The serious consideration of it dates from the organization of The Society for Psychical Research, founded in Cambridge, England, in 1882. Many eminent men have been connected with this organization. Among its presidents have been Professor Henry Sidgwick, Professor Balfour Stewart, Arthur J. Balfour, Professor William James, Sir William Crookes, Sir Oliver Lodge, Professor Richet, and Professor W. F. Barrett, all names of high standing in science and philosophy. Other eminent men connected with it have been Alfred Russel Wallace, F. W. H. Myers, Richard Hodgson, W. F. Stead, and Andrew Lang. At the head of The American Society for Psychical Research, an offshoot of the English society, was the late Professor James H. Hyslop, and other noted American students of the subject are Henry Holt, Booth Tarkington and H. Addison Bruce. A noted representative in England is A. Conan Doyle. *The Scientific American* recently (1922) appointed a committee of eminent experts to investigate the subject and offers large money prizes to any one who will produce supernormal phenomena to their satisfaction. Several fraudulent attempts to win the prize have already been exposed and the present outlook (November, 1924) is not promising.

The aim of these societies and investigators is to apply the most scientific methods and tests to such subjects as hypnotism and trance, telepathy, ghosts and apparitions, and especially to alleged spirit communications of all kinds. They have carried on an immense amount of inquiry, examined hundreds of cases in many lands, and published a large literature, including many volumes and reports. They have given out little as established results, but as early as 1884 the English society felt justified in affirming: "Our society claims to have proved the reality of thought-transference—of the transmission of thoughts, feelings, and images from one mind to another by no recognized channel of sense."

The subject is a legitimate one for scientific inquiry and urgently calls for it. It falls within the field of human experience and belongs to science and psychology, and therefore it is subject to the same means and methods of investigation as other fields of experience. And the intense practical interest and importance of the subject make such inquiry pressing and imperative.

No question can be raised against the competency, honesty and sincerity of these investigators. Their mere names, so well-known and eminent, stamp them as men of conspicuous ability and high logical training and skill. Their only motive is the sincere desire to know the truth. They have no preformed theories on the subject to support, and they have endeavored to prosecute their inquiries with caution and candor, fairness and impartiality.

No general denial can be logically entered against the possibility of communications from departed spirits. Neither physical science nor psychology nor religion has any ground on which, or any interest for which, to make such a denial. To enter a general negative on this subject is utterly unscientific. It is to decide a question before it has been examined and the evidence heard. It would require enormous and practically omniscient knowledge to affirm that such communications cannot take place. The most any one can affirm is that to his mind no such communications have been proved. Huxley said that the question of miracles is one of simple historical fact and could not be decided by any general principle, and this question is a parallel case. The universe is too vast and mysterious and contains too much unexplored ground for us with our finite minds and limited experience to close the door against such communications. It will ever contain infinitely more things than are dreamt of in our philosophy.

The charge that such alleged communications consist of trickeries and trivialities calls for discrimination. This charge does lie against commercial spiritualism. The whole business of mercenary mediums is a mass and mess of fraud and frivolous deceptions, and every one should be warned against their wiles. Much harm has been done, especially to people of nervous temperament, by these impostors. But the investigations and results of the psychical researchers are of a different stamp. They are conducted with honest intentions and rigorous methods and are worthy of respect. Even the charge that all these alleged communications are trivialities does not hold, for some of them are remarkable and impressive and do not seem unworthy. There are many false miracles, but these do not annul the genuine ones; and the fraud connected with mercenary spiritualism does not invalidate any truth that may be in these psychical manifestations.

As to this truth, let every one be fully persuaded in

147

his own mind. These investigators have undoubtedly brought to light facts that are abnormal and mysterious and may mean much. They are, however, far from being agreed as to the explanation of these facts. Some of them, like Mr. Myers, Mr. Hodgson, Sir Oliver Lodge, Professor Hyslop and A. Conan Doyle, have been fully and finally convinced of the reality of communications from departed spirits; others of them, like Professor James, have been convinced of supernormal or inexplicable facts, but have remained unconvinced as to their being spirit communications; still others, like H. Addington Bruce, explain them by telepathy or other abnormal psychology; and other eminent scientific men, like Professor Edward Clodd, deny and flout the whole possibility of interworld communications.

The late Professor N. S. Shaler, of Harvard University, whose writings, especially his *The Individual: Study of Life and Death,* show him to have been one of our profoundest, calmest and most judicious scientific thinkers, says on this subject: "The only direct evidence that can claim scientific inquiry, which goes to show the persistence of the individual after death, is that afforded by the so-called occult phenomena; by the alleged appearance of spirits, or the communication with what appear to some inquirers to be the minds of the departed. Notwithstanding their urgent disinclination to meddle with or be meddled by the problems of spiritualism, the men of science have a natural interest in the inquiries of the few true observers who are dredging in that turbid sea. Trusting to the evident scientific faithfulness of these hardy explorers, it appears evident that they have brought up from that deep sea certain facts which, though shadowed by doubt, indicate persistence of the individual consciousness after death. It has, moreover, to be confessed that these few, and as yet imperfect, observations are fortified by the fact that through all the ages of his contact with Nature man has firmly held to the notion that the world was peopled with disembodied individualities which could appeal to his own intelligence. Such a conviction is itself worth something, though it be little; supported by any critical evidence it becomes of much value. Thus we may fairly conjecture that we may be on the verge of something like a demonstration that the individual consciousness does survive the death of the body by which it was nurtured."

One who has had no experience of such communications will not be easily convinced of their reality; but one can see no ground on which to close the door against them. We know only in part, an infinitesimal part, and the little circle of our light impinges on a vast rim of outlying darkness. We may well believe that we have yet undeveloped resources which in the future may lead to discoveries as marvelous to us now, could they be revealed to us, as our present wonders would have been to our ancient ancestors, could they have foreseen them. Wireless communications alone should make us wary in setting bounds to our powers, whether physical or spiritual. Christian faith surely has no interest in denying spirit communications, but should rather welcome them, if they were authenticated. Such a revelation and confirmation of the great hope would undoubtedly bring profound relief and comfort to many minds.

Our faith in immortality does not rest on the foundation of these alleged interworld communications. Leslie Stephen said that he would rather trust "the majestic doubt of our natural hope of immortality than these ghostly voices," and not a few would sympathize with him in this sentiment. The natural hope, which is grounded in the constitution of man as being related to a larger world so that the human spirit is ensphered in eternity, retains its assurance, and we also have a more sure word of prophecy in all the teachings and testimonies of revelation, sealed by the character and affirmation and resurrection of Christ. And yet who shall say that more light may not yet break forth to illumine and confirm the great hope?

3. *Has It Stood the Test of the Great War?*

How has the belief in immortality stood the test of the Great War? Has it gone down in the general convulsion and crash that seemed to undermine and sweep into ruin the whole fabric of our civilization? In answer to this question several things may be said.

For one thing the Great War, while it put a heavy, put no new, strain on our faith in God and immortality. The world has always been in a state of eruption, and if any war, however great, could have destroyed this faith it would have perished and passed away long ago. War at the worst is hardly ever a mere mad welter of wickedness and waste, but has a place in the larger plan of God and sometimes out of its lava bloom new and fine flowers of civilization.

> In this broad earth of ours,
> Amid the measureless grossness and the slag,
> Enclosed and safe within its central heart,
> Nestles the seed perfection. —*Whitman.*

For another thing, the general experience of men has been that great trials and even the greatest disasters confirm rather than destroy faith. Hebrew prophets and psalmists in the midst of tragic disasters and sorrows rose above them in their faith and uttered sublime declarations of trust, such as, "Clouds and darkness are round about him: Righteousness and justice are the foundation of his throne." The heroic soul of man often meets appalling calamities in this spirit of unfaltering trust. In the darkest night of despair the stars of faith flash out. Great crises call forth the deepest and most primal needs and powers of men, and then they rise to the supremest heights of faith and achievement. A great battle is a challenge to win a great victory.

The Great War has been the greatest call to faith and courage the world has ever heard. If there were no God to give meaning to it all and lead men to some worthy outcome, then the world is only a crazy ant-hill disturbed by the thrust of a sword and is the wildest absurdity of a disordered dream. Men fly to God in such an hour as their refuge and strength, a very present help in trouble.

This has been the effect of the war in a large degree upon the faith of men. This effect perhaps was greatest in the trenches, where the need was most terrible and most intensely realized. It was commonly said that there were no atheists in the trenches and that one had to go far back where it was safe before he would find any sceptics. The evidence on this point was abundant and accumulated in countless private letters and personal testimonies and published articles and volumes. The Great War has not weakened faith in immortality but

151

rather strengthened it. In its darkest hour we could not believe that our sons were marching into its fiery crater and being swallowed up and disappearing forever. Rather we believed with unflinching faith that every battlefield opened the door for hundreds and thousands, not into endless night, but into eternal morning.

Faith grows brighter in the friction and fires of trial and sorrow. The electric current becomes a glow of light, not as it slips with unhindered ease and smoothness along the wire, but only when it encounters the resistance of the filament in the lamp. Paul's spirit blazed up in glory when it struck the thorn in his flesh, and even the Son of God was made perfect through suffering so that his cross became his noblest crown. We cannot reach this prize through any easier process.

Our faith in immortality is one of our most precious products that comes high in price, and we must still fashion its crown in the furnace fires of this world.

> Only the prism's obstruction shows aright
> The secret of the sunbeam, breaks its light
> Into the jeweled bow from blankest white;
> So may a glory from defect arise.
>
> —*Browning.*

> Had he not turned us in his hand, and thrust
> Our high things low and shook our hills as dust,
> We had not been this splendor, and our wrong
> An everlasting music for the song
> Of earth and heaven.

4. *Has It Practical Value in Daily Life?*

This is the final pragmatic test and our question must submit to it. There are extreme views on both sides.

Dr. James H. Leuba in his book on *The Belief in God and Immortality,* in which he reports his statistical questionnaire already referred to, says outright that this belief is not good but bad in its effects. "The modern belief in immortality," he says, "costs more than it is worth. . . . Its disappearance from among the most civilized nations would be, on the whole, a gain. It would be difficult to evaluate the harm done to humanity in the past by the conviction that the real destination of man is the world to come." Of course this is only his personal opinion, and it counts for one.

The position of another eminent psychologist, Dr. G. Stanley Hall, is most peculiar. While positively and repeatedly in his books repudiating any personal belief in and desire for immortality, yet he strongly insists on its pragmatic value and necessity. "Every degree, even the slightest," he says, "of increased faith in a future eternal life of rewards and punishments for the soul gives inestimable support to morality." And again: "No one who knows the human heart can have patience with those who, because there are a few pure and lofty souls that can live out the best within them without the aid of hope or fear for the future, argue that more harm than good was done by these immense powers to stimulate righteousness and repress evil." So he writes in his *Jesus, the Christ, in the Light of Psychology.*

Yet in his later book, *Senescence,* in which he again argues for the pragmatic value of belief in immortality for the young, as he closes the last chapter but one he advises his young readers not to go on and read the final chapter on "The Psychology of Death," which is black as Egyptian night with pessimism. Here are his remarkable words of advice: "And so I am grateful to senescence that has brought me at last into the larger light of a new day which the young can never see and should never be asked to see. Thus if any of them should ever read my book thus far I would dismiss them here and in the following chapter address myself to the aged alone"! By telling his young readers that they should not go on into the next chapter could he have hit upon any surer device to make it certain that they would go on and read that chapter, even though they read no other? But what sort of truth is it that is true for the aged but not for the young? And can it be that nature has so constituted us that in order to live well we must believe in early life that something is true which in later life we must believe is false? If this is psychology, then the less of it the better. We may leave these two eminent psychologists to refute each other and pass on.

The opposite extreme from this view is the averment that without this faith there could be no worth and virtue in our human life at all. Religion and morality and all decency would disappear with it and we would all plunge into the ditch. Some religious thinkers and writers have boldly gone to this extreme. But nature is too orthodox to permit this. She has laws which she executes and on the lowest levels of human life maintains a necessary degree of morality. The Ten Commandments of Moses did not originate in principle with him, but go back to the cave man. Many utter agnostics as to immortality exhibit fine character and lead noble lives, and if this faith were generally lost the world would go on.

But would it go on just the same? This is the question. We cannot think it would. The loss of this faith from our life would sooner or later change our whole view of the value of life. It would at once cut off the great vision and motive of the future world and confine life to the near horizon and short time of this world, and to this disastrous result many agnostics, such as Huxley, John Stuart Mill and, as we have just seen. Dr. G. Stanley Hall bear striking testimony. All thoughts and feelings and motives springing from the permanent value of life and its eternal reward and retribution would cease to influence us, and we would think and act only as the creatures of a day. The majestic front of eternity would vanish and leave only ephemeral time. Our life could scarcely rise higher than eating and drinking to sustain the flesh which would presently become dust. We could not hide from ourselves the fateful fact that we are only animals and differ from them only in consisting of a little finer clay and richer blood. There would be in us no vital difference in kind from the beasts of the jungle and the insects of a summer evening, which, though born in the morning, yet grow old and die with the sunset. Our pride may cry out against this view, but its logic is inevitable.

It is doubtless true that the general loss of this faith would not immediately produce any great moral decline and disaster or even any noticeable difference, for it takes time for some causes to work out their effects. The swift express train continues its motion for some distance after the steam has been shut off in the locomotive, carried forward by its own momentum; but presently it slows down and stops. The furnace continues to give forth heat for a considerable time after the fire has been put out. Disease may not show serious symptoms at first and it may take a long time to develop, but it ends in death. Human society would continue its course with little change for a time, if it were to lose this faith.

But let time do its work and this unfaith bring forth its proper fruit, let the momentum of the old morality be spent, saturate society for ten generations or a thousand years with the belief that death ends all, and who shall say there will be no serious results, even social disintegration and disaster? There can be little doubt that the tendency of unbelief in this doctrine, or of positive belief that death is the end of life, is towards practical materialism. The gospel of this view is, Let us eat and drink, for tomorrow we die. However a few souls of fine fiber and heroic temper would resist this tendency, yet this is its logic, and it has no high motive and permanent value with which to oppose it.

Men will soon minimize and disregard consequences when they believe that all consequences will soon be over. The judgment of Emerson, who cannot be suspected of any undue leaning toward orthodoxy, is of peculiar weight on this point: "No sooner do we try to get rid of the idea of Immortality—than Pessimism raises its head. . . . Human griefs seem little worth assuaging; human happiness too paltry (at the best) to be worth increasing. The whole moral world is reduced to a point. Good and evil, right and wrong, become infinitesimal, ephemeral matters. The affections die away— die of their own conscious feebleness and uselessness. A moral paralysis creeps over us." And Ernest Renan said: "The day in which the belief in an after life shall vanish from the earth will witness a terrific moral and spiritual decadence. Some of us might do without it, provided only that others hold fast. But there is no lever capable of raising an entire people if once they have lost faith in the immortality of the soul."

On the other hand, the belief in immortality has the general voice of human experience and the course of history to bear witness to its value and moral necessity. This testimony finds a voice in practically all religions; it is pathetically but unmistakably evidenced in the earliest graves of men, it is painted on Egyptian coffins and cut on innumerable monuments under every sky, it is written in all the bibles of the world, and it is expressed in universal literature and art. The prophets, priests, apostles and martyrs of humanity have proclaimed it and sealed it with their blood. Men have died for it. And countless millions have been sustained ᵢv it through temptations, trials, sorrows, through all the tragedies and blood and tears of this world and have died triumphantly in its hope. Literally this faith in multitudes of believers has abolished all fear of death and turned this last great enemy into an angel of light to bear them home.

Definite instances of the effect of this faith can be given, cases that comply with all the conditions of scientific experiment and test. The following remarkable instance is given by Rev. Dr. Charles L. Slattery in his book on *The Gift of Immortality:* "The late F. W. Myers, through interest in psychic research, became convinced, in what he thought a scientific way, that life goes on after death. It was with him a hope, a trust, a faith; it was what he believed to be full evidence tested by the senses. With the manner by which he gained this assurance I now have nothing to do. You may think that he was grossly self-deceived. All I insist upon is that you grant that in Myers you have an example of a man who had suddenly awakened to a genuine conviction of immortality. Now, what difference did this conviction make? Let his friend William James give the answer: 'Myers's character . . . grew stronger in every particular. . . . Brought up on literature and sentiment, something of a courtier, passionate, disdainful, and impatient naturally, he was made over again from the day when he took up psychical research seriously. He became learned in science, circumspect, democratic in sympathy, endlessly patient, and above all, happy. The fortitude of his last hours touched the heroic, so completely were the atrocious sufferings of his body cast into insignificance by his interest in the cause he lived for. When a man's pursuit gradually makes his face grow handsome, you may be sure it is a worthy cause. . . . Myers kept growing handsomer and stronger-looking.' This is an illustration of what must happen to every man when, for one reason or another, he passes from no faith, or a conventional faith, in immortality into a robust and vital faith. It makes a difference in life."

One other instance we adduce from Dr. Slattery: "Of modern biographies there is not a more inspiring life than that of Louis Pasteur. His biographer says plainly that Pasteur was constantly mindful of immortality. 'Absorbed as he was,' is the record, 'in his daily task, he yet carried in himself a constant aspiration towards the Ideal, a deep conviction of the reality of the Infinite and a trustful acquiescence in the mystery of the universe.' Again the biographer writes: 'Absolute faith in God and in eternity, and a conviction that the power for good given to us in this world will be continued beyond it, were feelings which pervaded his whole life.' And at the end the biographer relates that it seemed as if 'Pasteur already saw those dead ones who, like him, had preserved absolute faith in the Future Life.' "

We may say, with the author of the Epistle to the Hebrews: "And what shall I more say? for the time would fail me to tell of Gideon, Barak, Jephtha; of David and Samuel and the prophets, who through faith subdued kingdoms, wrought righteousness, obtained promises, stopped the mouths of lions, quenched the power of fire, escaped the edge of the sword, from weakness were made strong, waxed mighty in war, turned to flight armies of aliens. Women received their dead by a resurrection: and others were tortured, not accepting deliverance; that they might obtain a better resurrection: and others had trial of mockings and scourgings, yea, moreover, of bonds and imprisonment: they were stoned, they were sawn asunder, they were tempted, they were slain with the sword: they went about in sheepskins and goatskins; being destitute, afflicted, ill-treated (of whom the world was not worthy), wandering in deserts and mountains and caves, and the holes of the earth. And these all, having had witness borne to them through their faith, received not the promise, God having provided some better thing concerning us, that apart from us they should not be made perfect."

Dr. Slattery sums up and concludes his chapter on the responsibility that immortality lays on the individual in the following striking passage: "Immortality throws on the individual at least four commanding responsibilities:

the responsibility to be master of himself in all temptations; the responsibility to be courageous in all the hard places of experience; the responsibility to detach himself from the mere things of life; and the responsibility to buckle himself to a task so great that only eternity is long enough to complete it. If he fulfills these responsibilities he has already passed from death into endless life. He already stands firmly in the high and beautiful country of immortality."

"Where there is no vision the people perish." Seen at a distance the main range of the Rocky Mountains is a glorious sight. The planet is wrinkled into those giant billows of rock that rise above the sea level at some points three miles high. Their sides and summits are robed in unsullied snow, splendid white visions with their bases buried in the molten heart of the globe and their peaks plunged into the sun. The sight gives one a sense of power and grandeur, majesty and mystery that almost impels one to break forth in a shout to give relief and expression to his mystic emotion.

And yet the question arises, What use is that mountain range? No grain of wheat or blade of grass ever grows up there, and no foot treads those icy heights. Cubic miles of rock and billions of tons of ice and snow are heaved up in those ridges against the sky: why all this waste? A mercenary mind would calculate the amount of wealth in coal and silver and gold stored up in them and would estimate the profit that might be realized if they were torn down and spread out over the plains.

Yet there is no waste in those mountains but they are of great use in many ways. He who built all things knew what he was doing in pushing up those summits and planting them on their immovable foundations. They are storehouses of life. All summer long those vast snowdrifts and glaciers spin themselves into slender rills which gather into streams and leap over precipices, dissolving into iridescent mist and weaving exquisite rainbow-colored bridal veils around waterfalls, and converge into rushing roaring cataracts and rivers and flow out over the plains in steady irrigation. Those snowy summits fling far and wide meadows and orchards and wheat fields, towns and cities, turning deserts into gardens and peopling them with multitudes. Denver is a daughter of those snows. Vast populations suckle life from those immaculate breasts.

Not only so, but those rocky ribs of the earth play a great part in the life of the continent, determining the course of winds and rivers, reaching up with their giant icy hands and squeezing the moisture out of the clouds from the Pacific and pouring it as rain upon distant plains and breathing fresh vitalizing air over the whole land. Level those barren heights and cities would perish and the Mississippi Valley would in large part become a desert. The great bread basket of the continent would fill up with sand and rock. Everything in nature is beautiful in its time, and those gigantic ridges, that we may have thought useless and that a mercenary calculator would want to tear down and turn to material profit, are the shining hills of God whence he sends down streams of life upon the earth.

Even so are the spiritual verities and eternities of the world such mountain heights. To dim worldly vision they may seem cold and barren, yielding no fruit or profit and tempting only visionary eyes and foolish feet.

161

But they are the mountains of God, the mother of all high and fine life and beauty and blessedness, the fountain of streams that are for the healing of the nations and the satisfaction of the deepest thirst of the human soul, irrigating waters that cause the earth to grow green and the wilderness and the solitary place to be glad and the desert to rejoice and blossom as the rose. We would level these spiritual heights at our peril. All the higher and finer things of life would go down with them, and then could we say, with Walt Whitman,

Let the earth desert God, nor let there ever henceforth be mention'd the name of God!
Let there be no God!
Let there be money, business, imports, exports, custom, authority, precedents, pallor, dyspepsia, smut, ignorance, unbelief!

Immortality is one of these majestic heights. Some eyes are so dim or blind that they fail to see any such shining summit and may think, seriously and even sadly, or lightly and frivolously, that it is all a cloud-land mist or subjective illusion and delusion. But faith sees it and lives under its mighty spell and drinks of its streams and finds in its refreshing water life more abundant, sweeter and richer and pulsing with eternal hope. Faith sees it as it sees all the great and beautiful and blessed things in life.

5. *The Alternatives of Immortality.*

In forming our decision on any subject we should consider the alternatives. It is not wise to tear down the old house before we have a new house built. The old habitation may be only a hut altogether inadequate and uncomfortable, but it may be better than going out into storm and night. The consequences of a decision may react upon and modify, if not reverse, our sense not only of its expediency but of its fundamental truth and right. In the field of moral truth there is a subjective element that enters into and helps to create the belief we form. We must make our ideals come true, and "the will to believe" thus turns our faith into fact. The alternatives to immortality should have their proper influence in determining our attitude towards it. Our moral and religious nature has its ineradicable and insuppressible rights in the matter, and it will declare its needs and cast its vote. We should therefore face the alternatives of immortality before deciding against it. This is a legitimate part of our pragmatic test of the doctrine.

Faith in immortality is so intertwined with faith in a personal God that if we give up the one we shall not long be able to keep the other. The two practically stand together, and if we abandon the hope of immortality we shall find ourselves in an atheistic world and starless night. The specter of such a world is so destructive of all reason and right, faith and hope, and is so fearful that the soul shrinks from it in horror. The atheistic or pantheistic Absolute has been described as "an immense solitary specter—it hath no shape, it hath no sound, it hath no time, it hath no place. It is, it will be, it is never more nor less, nor sad nor glad. It is nothing—and the sands fall down in the hourglass, and the hands sweep around the dial, and men alone live and strive and hate and love and know it."

No sadder or more terrible words have ever been written than the confessions of atheists and agnostics in describing the world as they see it. In the last paragraph of the last book Herbert Spencer wrote, he leaves the following as his last message to the world: "And then comes the thought of this universal matrix itself, anteceding alike creation and evolution, whichever be assumed, and infinitely transcending both, alike in extent and duration; since both, if conceived at all, must be conceived as having beginnings, while Space had no beginning. The thought of this blank form of existence, which, explored in all directions as far as imagination can reach, has, beyond that, an unexplored region compared with which the part imagination has traversed is but infinitesimal—the thought of a Space compared with which our immeasurable siderial system dwindles to a point, is a thought too overwhelming to be dwelt upon. Of late years the consciousness that without origin or cause infinite Space has ever existed and must ever exist, produces in me a feeling from which I shrink." And so the philosopher, who declared in his *First Principles* that religion "concerns us more than any other matter whatsoever," finally sat looking out into blank space in which there twinkled no star of hope. It is a sad and pitiful outcome of so ponderous and pretentious a system of philosophy.

John Tyndall, the eminent physicist, who was so near to materialism in his philosophy, confessed: "I have noticed through years of self-observation that it is not in hours of clearness and vigor that this doctrine commends itself to my mind; for in the presence of stronger and healthier thought it ever dissolves and disappears as offering no solution of the mystery in which we dwell and of which we form a part."

Among his last words David Friedrich Strauss wrote:

164

"In the enormous machine of the universe, amid the incessant whirl and hiss of its jagged iron wheels, amid the deafening crash of its ponderous stamps and hammers, in the midst of this whole terrific commotion, man, a helpless and defenseless creature, finds himself placed, not secure for a moment that on an imprudent motion a wheel may seize and rend him, or a hammer crush him to powder."

It was of such a world that Jean Paul Richter dreamed in his *Dream of a World Without God:*

I dreamed I was in a churchyard at midnight. Overhead I heard the thunder of distant avalanches and beneath my feet the first footfalls of a boundless earthquake. Lightning gleamed athwart the church windows and the lead and iron frames melted and rolled down. Christ appeared and all the dead cried out, "Is there no God?" And Christ answered, "There is none. I have traversed the worlds, I have risen to the suns, with the milky ways I have passed athwart the great waste spaces of the sky: there is no God. And I descended to where the very shadow cast by Being dies out and ends, and I gazed out into the gulf beyond and cried, 'Father, where art thou?' But answer came none, save the eternal storm which rages on. We are orphans all, both I and you. We have no Father." Then the universe sank and became a mine dug in the face of the black eternal night besprent with thousand suns. And Christ cried, "Oh, mad unreasoning Chance: Knowest thou—thou knowest not—where thou dost march, hurricane-winged, amid the whirling snow of stars, extinguishing sun after sun on thy onward way, and when the sparkling dew of constellations ceases to gleam, as thou dost pass by? How every soul in this great corpse-trench of a universe is utterly alone?" And I fell down and peered into the shining mass of worlds, and beheld the coils of the great Serpent of eternity twined about these worlds; and these mighty coils began to writhe and then again they tightened and contracted, folding around the universe twice as closely as before; they wound about all nature in thousand folds, and crushed the worlds together. And all grew narrow and dark and terrible. And then a great immeasurable bell began to swing and tell the last hour of time and shatter the fabric of the universe, when my sleep broke up and I awoke. And my soul wept for joy that I could still worship God—my gladness and my weeping and my faith, these were my prayer.

THE CHRISTIAN BELIEF IN IMMORTALITY

These visions of a world without God and an eternal starless night and storm are the alternatives to immortality. Over against these horrors we set the prospect and promise of him who said: "In my Father's house are many mansions; if it were not so, I would have told you; for I go to prepare a place for you. And if I go and prepare a place for you, I come again, and will receive you unto myself; that where I am, there ye may be also." Which of these two visions, the corpse-trench or the Father's house, makes the deepest and most convincing and compelling appeal to our total nature, mind and heart, instinct and reason, feeling and aspiration? The world has made no mistake in choosing the alternative of faith and hope.

> Cleave ever to the sunnier side of doubt,
> And cleave to Faith beyond the forms of Faith!
> She sees the Best that glimmers through the Worst,
> She feels the Sun is hid but for a night,
> She spies the summer thro' the winter bud,
> She tastes the fruit before the blossom falls,
> She hears the lark within the songless egg.
> —*Tennyson.*

Tried by the pragmatic test, whether applied by the psychologist, scientist, prophet and poet, or by Christian believer or by unbeliever, our faith in immortality stands confirmed and justified. It nourishes and sustains our highest life, and without its vision such life would wither and perish.

CHAPTER IX

SUMMARY AND CONCLUSION

We shall now gather up the lines of our argument and summarize and evaluate them.

1. *Summary*

I. The belief in immortality when reduced to its essential content means faith in the endless persistence of human personality after death, but does not involve conditions and details of that life that are necessarily beyond our experience.

Modern thought means the vast accumulated mass of knowledge in science and in all fields of investigation and especially does it mean the scientific spirit of truth-seeking. Faith in immortality must be brought into harmony with all other knowledge, for all truth is one in consistency, and it must submit to all the processes and tests by which we reach truth in ethical fields.

II. Modern thought meets us most impressively in science and philosophy. The vastness of the universe, the universal reign of law and the doctrine of evolution impinge upon this faith, but under reflection they fall into harmony with spiritual values and even turn the world into a congenial soil and atmosphere for this faith.

As to the concepts of philosophy, agnosticism refutes itself, materialism is discredited, pantheism contradicts

167

our intuition of personality, and personalism, the prevailing philosophy through the ages, is the very home of this hope.

III. The most powerful objection to immortality is the dependence of the soul on the body as though the two came into existence and perished together. But this objection has been undermined by the evidence that the soul is the formative agency of the body, molding and mastering it, and thereby showing that the soul may be wholly freed from the flesh in the crisis of death when it may be clothed upon with some other form of body.

IV. The natural grounds of belief in immortality are rooted in the nature of the human soul as reality in itself, which must conserve its living energy, and which is constituted as personality which is the highest expression and a permanent value of our world, and we therefore believe of all worlds.

V. The religious grounds of belief in immortality are rooted in the constitutional religious nature of man, the Fatherhood of God, the instinct of the heart, the incompleteness of the soul and of the world, and the prophetic elements in life.

VI. The distinctively Christian belief in immortality, recorded and transmitted in the New Testament, which modern criticism has confirmed as a trustworthy historical document, is rooted in the teaching, character, divinity and resurrection of Christ.

VII. Life maintains its continuity through harmony with its environment, and science and revelation unite in declaring that perfect correspondence with a permanent environment would be eternal life, and this condition will be realized in the eternal world.

SUMMARY AND CONCLUSION

VIII. The belief in immortality stands the pragmatic test when tried by various processes. The verdict of scientific men, while divided, is not hostile or even unfriendly on the whole. The question of spirit communications is open and subject to further investigation, but it must be left to the personal inquiry and experience of individuals. Trials and sorrows, such as the Great War, do not destroy this faith but bring its stars out in the night. And its logical and practical effect upon daily life is to lift it to higher visions and victories.

2. *Conclusion.*

When we come to the conclusion and evaluation of our arguments we must admit at the end as was admitted in the beginning of our discussion that we have not reached an indubitable demonstration and must still walk by faith. Yet it must surely be admitted that these arguments in their summation and cumulative force are impressively weighty. No one of them may be sufficient in itself to prove the certainty of this hope, but when taken together they so converge and mutually support one another that they combine to form a bundle hard to break, or a rope of many strands that will sustain the whole weight of our great faith. Though they may only reach probability, yet it is such a degree and strength of probability that we are willing to throw upon it our whole trust and life. As we have seen, we hardly ever reach any other kind of conclusion than probability, and yet once reached it is sufficient and decisive.

Ever on the high levels of life must we walk by faith and not by sight. Our sunlight is ever attended with shadows. The chessboard of the world is composed of bright squares alternating with dark, and we can see any great ethical and spiritual problem, in Browning's phrase, either as faith diversified with doubt, or as doubt diversified with faith. We would fain see it all bright, but it is not so constituted. Something is left to our individuality and sovereignty, ethical affinity and aspiration, personal decision and action. It is ever so. At one of the last appearances of the risen Christ to his disciples, "when they saw him, they worshiped him: but some doubted." Who shall penetrate to the secret of the individual will that turns the balance towards faith or doubt?

> Like you this Christianity or not?
> It may be false, but will you wish it true?
> Has it your vote to be so if it can?

It is not given unto us to live in a world of pure light, and the possibility of doubt is necessary to the possibility of choice and the development of personality and character. To know too much might be fatal to our higher interests, and "we know in part" in this world that we may be tested and fitted for the world where "we shall know even as we are known."

Obedience is ever a vital organ of spiritual knowledge. We know as we do, we get more light as we use the light we have, and faith and obedience grow together into clearer light and greater assurance. Revelation and psychology agree again on this point. "If any man willeth to do his will, he shall know of the teaching, whether it is of God, or whether I speak from myself." Professor James said that the universe "feels like a real fight," Donald Hankey says in his *Student in Arms:*

170

Second Series that "True religion means betting one's life that there is a God," and L. P. Jacks in his *Religious Perplexities* says that man "finds his own nature as hero exquisitely adapted to the nature of the universe as dangerous." Eternal life is not only a gift of God, but it is also a risk we must run, a battle we must fight, and an attainment we must achieve.

The question of immortality is one of these decisive battlefields of life. Whether we see it as dominant faith edged with doubt, or as dominant doubt edged with faith, is something that each one of us must decide for himself. God has given us sufficient light for us to exercise faith and left enough shadows for us to entertain doubt. Let every one be fully assured in his own mind, and to this personal decision must this question at last come.

Our intellectual reasonings on this subject will more or less influence us in our decision, but the deepest influences will come up out of our hearts and will be rooted in our life. Our decision will go far towards determining the kind of life we live, but the kind of life we live will go farther towards determining our decision. If we live as though death ended all, we shall easily drift into unbelief; but if we fight the good fight of faith and are mightily resolved to keep this great hope, its star will shine out in our sky and not fail us.

Eternal life, as we have seen, is not simply a future but also a present possession and experience. The future life, if it is to have value and interest for us, must be a prolongation of the essential elements and values of this life, and these values are Truth, Goodness and Beauty combined in perfect personality. The main business of this life is to develop and exercise and live this eternal life in this world without too much concern about the other world. We must find this life, as Wordsworth reminds us,

> in the very world which is the world
> Of all of us,—the place where in the end
> We find our happiness, or not at all.

It is possible to carry the spirit of otherworldliness to excess until it binds and smothers life in this world or reduces it to an unhealthy morbid consciousness that is neglectful of the proper things of this world. The ancient Egyptians did this beyond any other people of history. Tutankhamen stored his tomb with the costliest treasures of his kingdom, literally robbing the living to enrich the dead. He packed his sepulcher full of the symbols of the other world until it would hold no more; and however sincere his pathetic faith, he did this largely at the expense of his subjects and of his own life in this world.

We are not to repeat this mistake, though we are in little danger of it and though it may assume different forms with us. The other world is not to be thrust into this world so as to crowd out present duties and interests and joys. The sailor steers his ship by the sun and stars, but he does not keep looking at them all the time: if he did this he would surely wreck his ship. An occasional glance starward is sufficient to enable him to keep his reckonings and make his port.

Eternal life is correspondence with God in Christ in this world, and our main duty and delight should be to develop this increasingly rich and satisfying life in har-

172

mony and fellowship with him in all our ways, and an occasional glance in the direction of the eternal state will be sufficient. We must know that the stars of eternity are ever over us and that the harbor of the final world is waiting to welcome us, but too much thought about these may be diverting and distracting.

A wholesome life lives mainly in the present while only at intervals does it look ahead. This is true in friendship and government and even in business, and not less is it true in religion. Life is not mere lasting either in this world or in that which is to come. It is not a quantity so much as a quality. It is a timeless state. If we do not attain a life that is of essential worth in this world, there is small assurance of ever keeping it or having a right to it in the next world. Truth, Goodness and Beauty are timeless values and permanent possessions, and we can truly have hope of them hereafter only as we have them here. "We do not make them," says Dean Inge; "they are above us. It is rather they that make us immortal and blessed if we can lay hold of them and live them." If we live this life here in devotion to and development of these essential values we shall attain to imperishable personality; and then our life there shall be continuous with our life here, and we shall reap the good man's highest reward, the wages of going on.

Such a life will save us from morbid consciousness of the other world and will promote a healthy and vigorous and full-orbed life in this world; and it will also lift us above conceptions and hopes of a vulgar materialistic heaven. It carries in its own bosom the promise and pledge of its permanence in its own sense of eternal

173

worth; and though it may give little anxious thought to the hidden things that remain with God, yet will it be sure and serene and victorious in its assurance of the life immortal, being confident that it will be satisfied when it awakes in his likeness.

Gathering up all the threads of our discourse, following all gleams of light, listening to all voices and intimations of mind and heart, nature and revelation, science and Scripture, and letting our deepest needs and finest moods speak, we join in faith with Socrates as, taking the fatal hemlock, he said, "The venture is a glorious one"; with Carlyle in his "Everlasting Yea"; with Charles Frohman standing on the deck of the sinking *Lusitania* and saying as he went down, "Why should we fear death? It is the most beautiful adventure in life"; with Job as he affirmed, "I know that my Redeemer liveth and apart from my flesh I shall see God"; with Paul as he declared, "To die is gain"; and above all we trust the Lord of Life and Master of Death, who prayed, "Father, I desire that they also whom thou hast given me be with me where I am, that they may behold my glory."

In the presence of our modern thought, nowhere denied and at many points confirmed by it, our belief in immortality confidently persists and grows with all our growth. Reason and revelation, mind and heart, science and philosophy, faith and obedience, the high interests of this world and hope for the next, converge upon and meet in and are satisfied with belief in the life everlasting.

And I heard a voice from heaven saying, Write, Blessed are the dead who die in the Lord from henceforth: yea, saith the Spirit, that they may rest from their

SUMMARY AND CONCLUSION

labors; for their works follow with them. (Revelation 14:13.)

All we have willed or hoped or dreamed of good shall exist,
Not its semblance, but itself; no beauty, nor good, nor power
Whose voice has gone forth, but each survives for the melodist
When eternity affirms the conception of an hour.
—Browning.

Jerusalem the Golden!
　I weary for one gleam
Of all thy glory folden
　In distance and in dream!
My thoughts, like palms in exile,
　Climb up to look and pray
For a glimpse of that dear country
　That lies so far away.

Jerusalem the Golden!
　There all our birds that flew—
Our flowers but half unfolden,
　Our pearls that turned to dew,
And all the glad life-music,
　Now heard no longer here,
Shall come again to greet us
　As we are drawing near.
—Gerald Massey.

INDEX

Absolute, The pantheistic, 163.
Addison, quoted, 33.
Agnosticism, 39-40, 167.
Alger, William R., quoted, 83, 87, 96, 98.
Angell, President James R., 142.
Antares, 30.
Aristotle, 22.
Astronomy, The new, 20, 65.
Atoms, 14, 40.
Augustine, quoted, 80.

Balfour, A. J., quoted, 35, 42.
Barrett, Professor W. F., 145.
Bateson, Professor William, 37, 64.
Beauty, 64; as essential worth, 93-94; 131, 132-133, 171, 173.
Betelguese, 30.
Bible, The, and modern knowledge, 20; critical reconstruction of, 104-107.
Birkoff, Professor George D., 142.
Body, The, relation to the soul, 48-58.
Book of the Dead, Egyptian, 13.
Bowne, Borden P., 43.
Brain, relation to the mind, 50-53.
Browning, Mrs. Elizabeth Barrett, quoted, 66, 143.
Browning, Robert, quoted, 58, 78, 89, 90, 152, 170, 175.
Bruce, H. Addington, 145-148.
Burns, quoted, 101.

Cæsar, 66.
Campbell, President William W., 133.

Carlyle, quoted, IX, 174.
Christ, Jesus, his doctrine of immortality, 16; and truth, 22; his teaching, 108-109; his character, 109-112; his divinity, 112-113; his resurrection, 113-124; his demonstration of immortality, 124-126; his definition of eternal life, 130; the incarnation of God, 134; 174.
Cicero, 108.
Clodd, Professor Edward, 148.
Columbus, 26, 67.
Conklin, Professor E. G., 142.
Conservation, of energy, 61.
Coulter, Professor John M., 142.
Cromwell, 77.
Crookes, Sir William, 145.

Dana, James D., 141.
Dante, 77.
Death, survival of soul in, 70-71, 102; cause of, 145, 148.
Demosthenes, 66.
Descartes, 43, 141.
Doyle, Sir A. Conan, 145, 148.

Electrons, 40-42.
Eliot, George, quoted, 15.
Emerson, quoted, 47, 96-97, 156.
Energy, conservation of, 61-62.
Ether, The, 41.
Evolution, a revolutionary principle, 20; and immortality, 36-38, 71-75, 128, 141.

Fabre, J. H., quoted, 46.
Faith, fundamental in all our reasoning, 25-26; its power, 26-27; we walk by, 169-170.

177

INDEX

178

INDEX

Lotze, quoted, 25, 35, 141.
Luther, 26, 67.

Macaulay, quoted, 101.
Man, his rank and power, 32-33, 64-69; his instincts, 84-85.
Marshall, Alfred, quoted, 79.
Martineau, James, quoted, 77-78, 83, 98.
Massey, Gerald, 175.
Materialism, 42-43, 167.
Matter, cannot crush mind, 32-33; relation to mind, 40-42.
McCreery, J. L., quoted, 138.
McDougall, Professor William, 50.
Mill, John Stuart, quoted, IX, 110, 155.
Millikan, Robert A., 141, 143.
Mind, trustworthiness of human, 24; relation to matter, 40-42.
Mitchell, Dr. T. W., on multiple personalities, 75-76.
Münsterberg, Professor Hugo, 141.
Muspratt, Sir Max, 143.
Myers, F. W. H., 145, 148, 157-158.

Newton, 141.
Nicholson, J. W., quoted, 41.
Noumenon, and phenomenon, 60.

Obedience, the organ of spiritual knowledge, 170-171.
Omar Khayyám, quoted, 74.
Osborn, Henry Fairfield, 142.
Otherworldliness, 172.

Pascal, quoted, 25.
Pasteur, Louis, IX, 158-159.
Paul, quoted, IX, 58, 66; his Epistles, 106-107; 113; his witness to the resurrection of Christ, 116-117; 132, 174.

Personalism, 142, 163, 167.
Personality, nature, power and worth of, 63-78; multiple, 70.
Plato, 43, 77, 109, 141.
Pratt, Professor J. B., 50.
Pringle-Pattison, Professor, on conditional immortality, 19.
Probability, as a guide in life, 27.
Pupin, Michael I., 142.

Relativity, 14.
Religion, nature of, 64; ground of belief in immortality, 79-103.
Renan, Ernest, quoted, 156-157.
Research, Society for Psychical, American, 140, 145; English, 145-146.
Resurrection, of Christ, 113-124.
Richet, Professor, 145
Richter, Jean Paul, quoted, 165.
Romanes, George, quoted, 84.
Russell, Bertrand, quoted, 72.
Russell, E. S., quoted, 53.
Royce, Josiah, his view of immortality, 18, 43.
Ruskin, quoted, 98.

Science, American Association for Advancement of, 142.
Science, new, 19-20.
Scientific American, The, 145.
Shakespeare, 77, 96, 144.
Shaler, Professor N. S., quoted, 148-149.
Shelley, quoted, 78, 83.
Sidwick, Henry, 145.
Simpson, Professor James Y., on conditional immortality, 19; on the resurrection of Christ, 123; 141.
Slattery, Rev. Dr. Charles F., quoted, 157-160.
Sneath, E. Hershey, quoted, 86.
Socrates, 22, 77, 174.

179